Men, Masculinities, and Poverty in the UK

Sandy Ruxton

Oxfam

First published by Oxfam GB in 2002

© Oxfam GB 2002

ISBN 0 85598 490 2

A catalogue record for this publication is available from the British Library.

Available from:

Bournemouth English Book Centre, PO Box 1496, Parkstone, Dorset, BH12 3YD, UK
tel: +44 (0)1202 712933; fax: +44 (0)1202 712930; email: oxfam@bebc.co.uk

USA: Stylus Publishing LLC, PO Box 605, Herndon, VA 20172-0605, USA
tel: +1 (0)703 661 1581; fax: +1 (0)703 661 1547; email: styluspub@aol.com

For details of local agents and representatives in other countries, consult our website:
http://www.oxfam.org.uk/publications

or contact Oxfam Publishing, 274 Banbury Road, Oxford OX2 7DZ, UK
tel: +44 (0)1865 311 311; fax: +44 (0)1865 312 600; email: publish@oxfam.org.uk

Our website contains a fully searchable database of all our titles, and facilities for secure on-line ordering.

Published by Oxfam GB, 274 Banbury Road, Oxford OX2 7DZ, UK.

Printed by Information Press, Eynsham.

The photographs in this book are taken from the *Male Image Photopack*, published by Working With Men, and available from Working With Men, 320 Commercial Way, London SE15 1QN, UK (tel. 020 8308 0709), www.workingwithmen.org

Oxfam GB is a registered charity, no. 202 918, and is a member of Oxfam International.

Men, Masculinities, and Poverty in the UK

Oxfam GB

Oxfam GB, founded in 1942, is a development, humanitarian, and campaigning agency dedicated to finding lasting solutions to poverty and suffering around the world. Oxfam believes that every human being is entitled to a life of dignity and opportunity, and it works with others worldwide to make this become a reality.

From its base in Oxford, UK, Oxfam GB publishes and distributes a wide range of books and other resource materials for development and relief workers, researchers, campaigners, schools and colleges, and the general public, as part of its programme of advocacy, education, and communications.

Oxfam GB is a member of Oxfam International, a confederation of 12 agencies of diverse cultures and languages which share a commitment to working for an end to injustice and poverty – both in long-term development work and at times of crisis.

For further information about Oxfam's publishing, and online ordering, visit www.oxfam.org.uk/publications

For further information about Oxfam's development and humanitarian relief work around the world, visit www.oxfam.org.uk

Contents

Foreword

The recent high level of interest in men's behaviour has provoked the production of a plethora of books and reports, and the development of an increasing number of projects. Yet, very occasionally, someone writes with genuine insight, shedding light in corners where only disagreement existed. In Men, Masculinities, and Poverty in the UK, Sandy Ruxton has managed just that. In reviewing literature and offering 'snapshots of practice' in employment training, health, fatherhood, and violence and crime, Sandy provides an overview and recommendations for practitioners, managers, policy makers, and academics alike.

His starting point, as that of Oxfam GB who commissioned the report, is how men and women can work together against poverty and for gender equality in a way that addresses the needs of both sexes. While many writers in this field take refuge in some basic ideological positions (are men victims or perpetrators? are they better off, or worse off, than women? should we be generally supportive of men?); Sandy instead steers a skilful course through these too easily polarized approaches.

Readers, however experienced, will be stimulated by this well researched and argued report, which examines both the literature and practice through the original lens of poverty. While tackling poverty and social exclusion is at the heart of the Government's social policy agenda, relatively little attention has been devoted to the links between poverty and gender – and even less to those between poverty, men, and masculinities. This study is among the first to attempt to close this gap.

Too often reports lose momentum by the time they reach the conclusions and recommendations, or try to be too provocative or controversial. But Sandy maintains a coherent narrative, and is cautious but radical, in his approach. Readers may feel uncomfortable as they are encouraged to think through which groups of men need to be targeted; how far poverty contributes to the so-called 'crisis of masculinity'; and the extent to which a gender perspective underpins emerging practice with men. They will also be stimulated by thoughtful analysis and descriptions of more than 25 projects across the UK.

I would encourage anyone interested in work with men and gender studies – and particularly the links between policy and practice – to read this report. It provides a 'state of the nation' for those involved in developing work with men, and an accessible overview for others.

Trefor Lloyd,
Working With Men

Acknowledgements

I am very grateful to the many individuals and organisations who have contributed information, ideas, and advice for this study. Chief among them are David Bartlett (Fathers Direct), Alun Burge and Socrates Siskos (fpa Cymru), Colette Carol (CREST, Salford), Robert Cornwall (The Skills Centre, Gurnos, Merthyr Tydfil), Margaret Creer (Gingerbread), Colin Heyman (Recharge, Cardiff), Joy Higginson (Fathers Plus, Newcastle), Alastair Pringle (Men's Health Forum Scotland), Pippa Sargent (Campaign Against Living Miserably), and Richard Strittmater (Let's Get Serious, Hulme, Manchester).

I also wish to thank those who spoke at the Oxfam seminar to explore the project's interim findings: Peter Baker (Men's Health Forum), David Morran (Stirling University), Peter Moss (Thomas Corum Research Unit), and Sue Yeandle (Sheffield Hallam University). Several of them made useful comments on the text too, as did David Perfect and Helen Lindars (Equal Opportunities Commission).

Three individuals deserve particular thanks. Jill Mawson undertook research among projects in Scotland and provided much material for the study. Trefor Lloyd (Working With Men), who has done so much to promote work with men in the UK over the past decade or more, gave freely of his advice and insight and wrote the foreword. And Fran Bennett (Department of Social Policy and Social Work, Oxford University) dissected the text with her trusty red pen, and improved it in so many respects.

Thanks are also due to several members of Oxfam's staff, especially Sue Smith for managing the project throughout and Audrey Bronstein for supporting it. Ruth Emsley helped set up the seminar. Anna Coryndon edited the final text. Helpful comments at various stages of the draft were made by Caroline Sweetman, James Lang, Rachel Masika, and Kate Kilpatrick.

Finally, a number of male-dominated institutions (including schools, colleges, community projects, and prisons) have helped shape my understanding of men and masculinities over the years – but often in ways they perhaps did not foresee. To them I owe my gratitude too.

Sandy Ruxton

1
Introduction

Oxfam's approach to gender

Oxfam's principles apply across the gender divide – to allow women as well as men their essential dignity, and to work with women and men in its emergency and relief programmes in overcoming the pressures that exploit them. To achieve this, gender relations need to be transformed.

Oxfam's focus is on gender, rather than on women, to ensure that changing women's status is the responsibility of both sexes. It acknowledges that development affects men and women differently and that it has an impact on relations between men and women ...

Oxfam's Gender Policy (extract), May 1993

Oxfam has been working on gender as a key factor in development in its international programme since the early 1980s.[1] 'Gender analysis' is central to its understanding of the causes of poverty, and therefore to the effectiveness of solutions. Gender analysis explores and highlights the relationships of women and men in society, the inequalities in those relationships, and their causes. It involves examining the distribution of gender roles and responsibilities, and identifying the practical needs and strategic interests of men and women. It asks key questions such as: who does what; who has what; who decides; how; who gains; who loses? At the same time, gender analysis examines the likely impact of interventions not just on men and women as a whole, but on particular groups of men and women within these overall categories.[2]

In Oxfam's international work, gender analysis has tended to focus on developing programmes aimed directly at improving the lives of women, based on continuing evidence that they are the majority in the poorest groups in most countries, and developing countries in particular. In many developing countries, women earn on average only 60 to 70 per cent of what men are paid for similar work (and in parts of Africa and Asia, only

50 per cent). Women also work longer hours than men; in developing countries, women's work hours are estimated to exceed men's by about 30 per cent.[3]

Within this context, it has often been argued that devoting time and resources to work with men can prove counter-productive, given entrenched gender inequalities which leave men predominantly holding the reins of power. Furthermore, there have been fears that engaging more actively with men may reinforce the backlash against women's claims to equality that has occurred in recent years.

Yet although the widespread assumption that men in general are 'in crisis' is an exaggeration, the evidence outlined in this report suggests that, in the UK at least, life is increasingly insecure for many men. While men as a group do continue to hold structural power, and women remain the majority in the poorest groups, many men now face poverty and social exclusion too. Exploring the different ways in which particular groups of men and women are disadvantaged by economic and social change helps to deepen understanding of the increasingly complex reality of gender relations. It is therefore an essential prerequisite for developing appropriate analysis and action in response.

Aims of the report

Since the mid 1990s, Oxfam GB's UK Poverty Programme has been seeking to complement Oxfam's work in other countries, in response to a concern that the organisation should begin to address poverty 'at home' in a more systematic way.[4] Oxfam believes that a key component of poverty is powerlessness and the inability to influence relevant decision-making processes (sometimes described as a lack of 'voice'). Oxfam is concerned with poverty issues that go beyond income alone and focus on broader principles, including accountability and good governance; the promotion of human rights; diversity and anti-discrimination; and coherence between economic and social policies.

Gender analysis is fundamental to the work of Oxfam's UK Poverty Programme. As this report makes clear (see Chapter 2), gender relations are enacted differently at different times and in different places. Oxfam therefore decided to take a new look at gender and poverty in the UK and to explore three key issues. Firstly, which men suffer poverty and disadvantage, and under what circumstances? Second, do organisations that work with men have an understanding of gender analysis, and do they share Oxfam's approach? Third, in what ways (if at all) do these organisations focus on poverty, and do they share Oxfam's view that gender and poverty are connected?

Oxfam's international work is grounded in the understanding that poverty has many causes, and that the best solutions are holistic and integrated. We take the same approach in the UK, and therefore decided to investigate the experience of a wide range of community-based groups across Britain, in particular those working in the fields of employment training, men's health, gender-based violence, and fatherhood.

This report builds on previous work undertaken by Oxfam on gender and urban regeneration in the UK.[5] It explores how changing economic, social, and political circumstances are affecting gender relations. It also highlights the particular impact of poverty and social exclusion on working class men,[6] and identifies how gender analysis can be used to develop work with men across a range of sectors to promote gender equality. [7]

The objectives of the research project were:
- to identify examples of work with men suffering poverty and social exclusion in the UK, especially work based on a clear gender analysis;
- to review the related literature on men, masculinities, and poverty;
- to produce a UK-wide analysis of the nature, scope, and effectiveness of work with men which has an impact, direct or indirect, on poverty;
- to make recommendations for developing work with men in the UK, in order to address poverty and gender inequality.

It is intended that this report should both inform public debate in the UK and contribute to the development of Oxfam's work internationally around the theme of men and masculinities.

Structure of the report

Chapter 2 highlights key aspects of the available UK evidence on gender and poverty, outlines the main theoretical debates about men and masculinities, and explores the aims and tools of gender analysis.

Chapter 3 outlines the methodology used, including the primary research carried out, the secondary literature reviewed, and the consultation undertaken on the draft findings.

Chapter 4 explores the recent development of government policy to tackle poverty and social exclusion, the differential impact of such policy on men and women (especially those in the most disadvantaged groups), and the existing institutional mechanisms for promoting gender equality.

Chapter 5 surveys the impact of the changing labour market on men, examines the approach of employment-training projects to gender issues, highlights the particular needs of men at different ages, and identifies how greater gender-awareness could be developed.

Chapter 6 examines the evidence that men's health has been accorded insufficient attention, explores mental and sexual health issues among young men, and highlights initiatives to tackle men's broader health needs.

Chapter 7 analyses how far men are the perpetrators of violent – and in particular gender-based – crime, highlights attempts to challenge men's 'domestic' violence, and explores attempts to address the wider links between masculinity and offending.

Chapter 8 examines the contribution of fathers to contemporary family life, explores how services can engage with fathers most effectively, and highlights practical project initiatives and models of support for low-income fathers.

Chapter 9 concludes with a range of recommendations on improving the understanding of gender analysis; mainstreaming masculinity and gender; targeting male poverty; making masculinities visible; promoting good practice in working with men; increasing funding for work on masculinity issues; and furthering the research agenda.

The way forward

The report's findings will be taken forward within the context of a wider two-year project, which is being managed jointly by Oxfam's UK Poverty Programme and its Middle East/Eastern Europe/Confederation of Independent States regional programme, and co-funded by the Department for International Development. This project seeks to develop gender analysis, and to improve programme work and policy advocacy to tackle the impact of poverty on women and men. Based on a workshop bringing together representatives from several regions within Oxfam's global programme, outputs will include the publication of good-practice case studies and training modules during 2002 and 2003.

2
Men and masculinities: a poverty perspective

A crisis of masculinity?

Increasingly, boys and young men seem to have difficulty maturing into responsible citizens and fathers. Declining educational performance, loss of traditional 'male' jobs, the growth of a 'laddish' anti-social culture, greater use of drugs, irresponsible teenage fatherhood, and the rising suicide rate may all show rising insecurity and uncertainty among young men. This has worrying implications for the stability of family life and wider society. For example, recent research suggests that young men may not grow out of crime in their late teens as they were once assumed to do.

Home Office, 'Supporting Families: A consultation document', 1998
http://www.homeoffice.gov.uk/vcu/suppfam.htm

Public debate about a supposed 'crisis in masculinity' expanded significantly in the 1990s, and looks set to continue. In the UK, it is common to see media articles highlighting issues such as the educational underachievement of boys and the rise in suicides among young men. A similar trend is increasingly visible in official documents since the Labour government came to power, arguably reflecting a particular emphasis on men and masculinities within emerging gender policy.[1]

Yet these statistics are news largely because they appear to buck the dominant trends. As the Equal Opportunities Commission has recently demonstrated in its campaign to generate public debate around 'Sex Equality in the 21st Century',[2] on the vast majority of economic, social, and cultural indicators women, as a group, fare worse than men. This picture is confirmed by the publication by the Office for National

Statistics in 2001 of *Social Focus on Men*, which brings together for the first time official data on men's lives from a variety of sources. It concludes that:

> In many ways, men today live in a different world from that of their fathers. Family life has become more diverse, with cohabitation increasing and fewer men marrying than in the past. At one time, men were recognised as the primary providers of security and financial support for their family but this is no longer always the case as more women have entered the labour market. Nevertheless, differences in circumstances between the genders remain: men have higher incomes; they outnumber women in management and in many professional occupations; and traditional roles in the home may still exist with women undertaking the bulk of domestic chores.[3]

Oxfam is aware through its international work that women suffer disproportionately from poverty relative to men, and that they are the majority in the poorest groups. This 'feminisation' of poverty has worsened over the past decade or more, and has therefore increased women's dependence and vulnerability.

This is also generally true in the UK. For example, women who work full-time earn on average 18 per cent less per hour than men who work full-time, and female part-timers earn 41 per cent less than male full-timers.[4] This is due to direct discrimination, occupational segregation (60 per cent of women workers are in the ten lowest pay categories such as catering, retail, and cleaning), and the concentration of women in part-time work.[5] Set alongside the lack of affordable childcare and the undervaluing of women's care work, many women remain in a position of relative economic insecurity and dependence.

To help explain this position, Connell introduces the useful concept of the 'patriarchal dividend', which suggests that men accrue benefits from unequal shares of the products of social labour and can 'call in' the dividend of belonging to the dominant sex whenever they like.[6] Reflecting this dividend, most statistics, policies, and interventions are shaped around an unspoken assumption of male dominance. In other words, men tend to have the structural advantage of setting the norm. In Britain, as elsewhere, it is usually when differing outcomes for men and women question this assumption that media interest is aroused.

Nevertheless, it is important to remember that neither men nor women are homogenous groups. The differences between men and women must be seen alongside the differences between groups of men and between groups of women, cross-cut by social class, race, age, disability, or sexual orientation. Cornwall rightly argues that '... not all men ... have power and not all of those who have power are men.'[7]

Picturing gender and poverty in the UK

Providing a valid statistical picture of gender and poverty is very difficult. This is partly because of the issues raised above. But there is also a constant danger that statistics can be presented in certain ways in order to 'prove' that men or women are worse off, and therefore most deserving of assistance, funding, or media attention. While there are clearly differences between men and women across a range of indicators, which must be addressed, crude attempts to reinforce the competing claims of one sex over another may ultimately damage the goal of increasing the awareness of the importance of working for gender equality.

So what do the statistics tell us about the position of poor men and women in the UK? Probably the most widely accepted evidence in relation to poverty is provided by the government's own annual Households Below Average Income (HBAI) figures. Where gender is concerned, however, it is important to note that the HBAI statistics attempt to measure the living standards of an individual as determined by household income. This assumes that both partners in a couple benefit equally from the household's income; an assumption which fails to take into account the evidence that, in practice, men tend to control more of the household income than women. In other words, HBAI may overestimate the position of women relative to men.

In addition, the HBAI excludes certain groups from the figures, including people living in residential institutions (such as hospitals, nursing homes, barracks, student accommodation, residential homes, and prisons), and homeless people or those in bed and breakfast accommodation. Given that significant numbers of men and women in poverty will be included within these populations (men in particular, in the case of homelessness and prisons), this means that the figures will also underestimate poverty.

It is often said that poverty is a women's issue, which of course does not mean that there are no poor men and boys (there are lots of them) but rather that women are disproportionately likely to be poor ...

M Howard, *et al.*, *Poverty: The Facts,* Child Poverty Action Group, 2001

Figure 1:
The risk of poverty for men, women, and children in 1990/2000
(defined as living below 50 per cent of mean income after housing costs)

20% | Men

24% | Women

34% | Children

Proportion living in poverty

Source: Department of Social Security, Households Below Average Income 1994/95- 1999/00. *Corporate Document Services, 2001*

Figure 1 takes as the poverty line the figure of 50 per cent of average (mean) disposable income after housing costs, a definition which is widely accepted by social statisticians.[8] This figure shows the risk of living in poverty for men and women in 1999 and 2000, and highlights the fact that, overall, men were less likely than women to live in low-income households. Figures from the same report demonstrate that men were also more likely to be in the top forty per cent of the income distribution than were women.

Particular groups were shown to be more likely to be at risk of poverty than others. The unemployed is the group with the highest risk, with nearly 80 per cent living in poverty. Sixty one per cent of individuals in lone-parent families (the vast majority of whom are women) live in poverty. The single-pensioner group, again dominated by women, is also vulnerable to poverty. While these statistics are not broken down by ethnic background, the report identifies that those from Pakistani and Bangladeshi families were particularly at risk of poverty too.

While the HBAI are the most commonly used figures, there are other ways of measuring poverty that should be considered. For example, the Poverty and Social Exclusion (PSE) Survey 1999,[9] conducted by a team of academics for the Joseph Rowntree Foundation, uses a consensual definition of poverty. This is based upon public perceptions of a range of items regarded as necessities, with an individual deemed to be poor if they lack two or more of these.

According to the PSE data, men have a 22 per cent chance of living in poverty, compared with 29 per cent for women. As the HBAI also reveal, particular groups are at greater risk; for instance, unemployed people (77 per cent), those on income support (70 per cent), and lone parents (62 per cent).

While limited specific information about gender and poverty is available, it can be extended by focusing on broader issues that can have an impact on, or be related to, poverty. In Box 1 we set out some key statistics based on the first ever overview of statistics on men produced by a UK government: *Social Focus on Men*. These have been chosen in particular to illustrate issues that are tackled in more detail in subsequent chapters of this report.

Despite the limited nature of the evidence presented in Box 1, it does illustrate that specific groups of men do indeed face disadvantage, especially as a result of economic restructuring over recent decades. Since the 1970s, large numbers of men in traditional industrial areas have become registered unemployed, or economically inactive due to long-term work-related health problems. And although once they are in work they are likely to earn more than women with the same qualifications, it is generally harder for working class men to get into the labour market than their female counterparts.

Behind high-profile concerns about a generalised 'crisis in masculinity', what we are therefore actually seeing is a contradictory picture, which reveals as many differences between men as between men and women. As Segal identifies:

> ... it is *particular* groups of men, especially unemployed, unskilled and unmarried men, who have far higher mortality and illness rates compared with other groups of men. Class, ethnicity and 'race', not gender, are the major predictors of educational failure, unemployment and crime.[33]

Working With Men/Paul Leatham

Box 1: Social Focus on Men: extracts from key findings

Income and employment

- Six in ten employees of working age in professional occupations are men, as are seven out of ten managers and senior officials.[10]

- Men's average gross income is higher than that of women, at all ages. In 2001 the average gross income for men who worked full-time in Britain was £490 per week compared with £367 per week for women.[11]

- Despite an increase in part-time working among men, only eight per cent of male employees work part-time, compared with 44 per cent of female employees.[12]

- The unemployment rate for men aged 16 and over was five per cent in Spring 2001. Around 20 per cent of unemployed men in their thirties and forties have been unemployed for three years or more, and this rises to nearly 25 per cent among those aged 50-64.[13]

- Men have higher unemployment rates than women across all age groups; however many women do not appear in the official unemployment statistics owing to their carer responsibilities.[14] Men from ethnic minority groups have higher unemployment rates than white men, and the highest rates are found among Caribbean and African men.[15]

Health

- Men have lower life expectancies than women, and the inequality in life expectancy between men in different social classes has widened over the last 20 years.[16]

- Although death rates for men are higher than those for women, women tend to have higher rates of morbidity,[17] and gender differences in mortality are greater in the most economically deprived areas. Over the last 30 years, death rates in the UK have fallen among most age groups; the exception being men in the 16-34 age group, for whom rates in 1999 were virtually the same as in 1971.[18]

- In 1999 suicide was the cause for around 25 per cent of deaths among men aged between 16 and 34 in the UK, and a further 35 per cent were caused by accidents.[19] Although suicide is three times more common among young men than young women, deliberate self-harm is three times more common among females. [20]

- Coronary heart disease is much more common among men than women: for men in all age groups between 35 and 74, the more deprived the area in which they live, the more likely they are to develop heart disease.[21]

- Historically, more men have tended to smoke cigarettes than women, although proportionately more men than women have given up smoking and rates for both sexes are now very similar.[22]

- More men than women exceed the government's current recommendation on daily alcohol consumption, and the proportion for men aged 16-24 is much higher than for other men.[23]
- Six in ten men are either overweight or obese, and the problem is even more marked among men aged 45 and over.[24]

Violence and crime

- Male offenders make up over 80 per cent of the total number of offenders in England and Wales. The number of male offenders peaks sharply in early adulthood, and then decreases with age. The pattern for female offenders is similar, but a lower proportion of females than males are offenders.[25]
- Over 33 per cent of all male offenders are cautioned or found guilty of theft and handling stolen goods. Crimes of violence are almost exclusively committed by men, though the total number of violent crimes is relatively small (just over ten per cent of all indictable offences).[26]
- Domestic abuse remains the most common form of violence experienced by women, but it accounts for only five per cent of incidents against men.[27]
- Around one in six of all incidents of criminal victimisation against Asians and African-Caribbeans is believed by the victim to be racially motivated; three in four victims describe the suspect as male.[28]
- Between January and June 2001, 745 homophobic incidents were reported to the Metropolitan Police, of which there were seven male victims for every female victim.[29]

Fatherhood

- Most mothers take greater responsibility for the care of children than fathers, and are more likely to be in employment than ever before. Men with children are more likely to be working – and working longer hours – than men without children.[30]
- In households with children under age 16, men report spending around three-quarters of an hour a day caring for and playing with their children; just under half the amount reported by women.[31]
- Almost 50 per cent of non-resident fathers say that they see their child every week, and only three per cent say they never see their child. Child maintenance is much less likely to be paid if the father is unemployed, and if he is under 20 years old when he first becomes a father.[32]

For further details, see *Social Focus on Men*, National Statistics, The Stationery Office, 2001

Figure 2:
The risk of poverty by family status in 1990/2000 (defined as living below 50 per cent of mean income after housing costs)

23%	Pensioner couple
33%	Single pensioner
23%	Couple with children
12%	Couple without children
61%	Lone parent
24%	Single without children

Proportion living in poverty

Source: Department of Social Security, Households Below Average Income 1994/95-1999/00. *Corporate Document Services, 2001*

Theoretical debates about men and masculinities

Gender politics is not just about standing up for women. It is about interrogating masculinity and the specifics of male experience, as well as femininity and female experience – acknowledging that gender (as opposed to sex) is constructed not natural or god-given. Feminists were the first to introduce a critical gendered perspective into 20th century political life. As feminist thought has evolved over the last three decades, the process of opening up ideas about men and problems associated with masculinity has been part of its own modernisation. This has included a growing certainty that social justice for women cannot be found in simply having more of what men have, but requires a transformation in men's lives too.

Anna Coote, Introduction to *New Gender Agenda,* Institute for Public Policy Research, Fabian Society, Fawcett Society, 2000

In order to fully understand the complexities and contradictions inherent in the picture painted above, it is important to be aware of the significant development of academic analysis in this field. During the 1990s in particular, interest in research on men has grown worldwide across a range of disciplines including health, education, and criminology, and a substantial body of literature has emerged.

In a recent publication for Oxfam GB, Chant and Gutmann have usefully summarised the arguments in favour of a stronger focus on men and masculinities, arguing that both men and women can gain from challenging the gender relations that oppress them.[34] They identify dangers in equating 'gender' with 'women', which can result in the entrenchment of static definitions of women (for example, as carers) and men (for example, as breadwinners). Furthermore, failure to engage with men often results in a greater burden of labour falling on women (frequently underpaid and undervalued, as in the case of childcare). Attempts to engage men in gender projects can encourage them to take greater responsibility for areas of concern such as violence, fatherhood, and sexual health. It can also help to undermine gender inequality.

Much of the research referred to above remains on a relatively abstract, and sometimes inaccessible level. In recent years, this more academic approach has tended to be overshadowed by popular psychology, as a result of works such as Robert Bly's *Iron John*,[35] and John Gray's *Men are from Mars and Women are from Venus*.[36] Books such as these have correctly identified emotional insecurity as a key theme for many men, especially middle class white men. However, they have also tended to reinforce the notion of gender difference, and to idealise a mythical pre-industrial past where men were supposedly more connected with their inner selves. On this basis, they have often justified arguments against advancement for women, and for a return to more traditional gender relations.

> Virtually all available research from the social and behavioural sciences suggests that women and men are not from Venus and Mars, but are both from planet Earth. We're not opposite sexes, but neighbouring sexes – we have far more in common with each other than we have differences.
>
> Michael Kimmel, *The Gendered Society*, Oxford University Press, 2000

Moving beyond simplistic 'essentialist' arguments such as these, new social research has in recent years developed more complex and subtle theoretical approaches. A central challenge for many writers has been that of making gender visible for men as well as women. Men as a group, in particular middle and upper class white men, hold a relatively powerful position in relation to women (and to other groups such as ethnic minorities, and gay men). They are not, however, aware of their privilege as *men*, and can therefore pretend that gender is unimportant. This continuing invisibility of masculinities means that the gendered standards that are held up as the norm appear to be 'gender neutral'.[37]

The use of the term 'masculinities' also conveys widespread acceptance that there is not one universal pattern of masculinity.[38] Gender is enacted differently within different cultures: the experience of an Afro-Caribbean working class male in inner London today would be very removed from that of a white working class male from a rural area. Sewell, for example, has explored the way in which young black men play out masculinities as collective responses to a racist culture, and how they therefore position themselves as 'superior' to whites and Asians in terms of their sexual attractiveness, style, creativity, and toughness.[39]

Collective masculinities are also defined within cultures and institutions beyond the individual, be it in the coal mine, the navy, or the print works.[40] And masculinities are actively 'produced' by individuals, using the resources and strategies available in a particular social setting, rather than being programmed by genes or fixed by social structures. Boys in school, for example, constantly negotiate and renegotiate their positions within peer groups, classes, and adult-child relationships.[41] The importance of what boys and men do in their relationships with women, children, and other men has led some to suggest that more emphasis should be placed on 'men's practices' rather than simply on 'masculinities'.[42]

Masculinities are dynamic too, changing according to specific historical circumstances.[43] The work of Connell has been especially influential here.[44] His widely used theory of 'hegemonic masculinities' suggests that particular forms of masculinity are dominant for a period of time until some form of crisis disrupts their power and stability. At present, in developed countries, hegemonic masculinities tend to be composed of a combination of economic success, racial superiority, and overt hetero-sexuality. At the same time, non-hegemonic forms of 'inferior' masculinity exist alongside, based on differences within and between men according to class, ethnicity, sexual orientation, and other characteristics. Connell has argued that, given the increasing pace of the process of globalisation, 'hegemonic masculinities' may also be evident in developing countries, but the extent to which gender relations converge is uneven.[45]

Connell's approach can be used to analyse the impact on men and masculinities of economic restructuring and unemployment in recent decades. During this period, some men have clearly increased their power, built upon factors such as the growth of transnational businesses, and the increasing circulation of images of masculinity based on competition and individualism (through sport, for example). Although not all men who are powerful have the characteristics of toughness and physical dominance associated with 'hegemonic masculinity', it remains important to their fantasy ideal. For men at the other end of the social scale, who have experienced 'downsizing' and 'retrenchment' and become unemployed, the outcomes in terms of poverty, stress, and loss of social support have often been serious.

> ... the experiences of women and men in the face of unemployment
> need not be all that different. If they do differ this may be as much to
> do with the hierarchical way in which labour markets are organised,
> the widespread and deep-rooted character of patriarchal assumptions
> about men and work and women and the home and wider structures
> of gender inequalities. Men *are* discovered in the analysis of
> unemployment but men as different from each other, in some cases,
> as they are different from women.
>
> D.H.J. Morgan, *Discovering Men*, Routledge, 1992

The responses of working class men to these shifting challenges to their masculinity vary significantly. While many adapt relatively well to the new circumstances they face, some turn to hostile attitudes and violence towards other disadvantaged groups (such as women, ethnic minorities, and gays) in a search for scapegoats. Others turn their frustration on themselves, generating rising suicide rates, especially among young men. Some lapse into passivity, existing on long-term sickness and disability benefits.

It is sometimes argued – and this approach lies at the heart of many traditional approaches – that, being 'natural', masculinity is impervious to reform. But the research outlined briefly above demonstrates the reverse. Dominant ideas of what masculinity is have been shown to be subject to change, linked in particular to shifts in power and politics.

Clearly there are risks involved in attempts to reshape masculinity. The emergence of 'men's movements', for example, could result in the shoring up of traditional gender roles and stereotypes, rather than their renegotiation. Yet as this report seeks to demonstrate, fledgling initiatives – albeit often small-scale and struggling – do exist, which are helping some men to build positive identities for themselves, whether as workers or carers. The challenge is to ensure that these are rooted in solid gender analysis, and replicated more widely.

> The status of 'men' as a (the) dominant social category remains virtually unchanged and may even have become intensified in some respects. One of the many paradoxes of men's situation is the combination of some men's structural power and some men's social exclusion, even when they themselves may enact power in their own lives.
>
> Jeff Hearn, 'The naming of men: national and transnational perspectives', in 'Promoting gender equality worldwide', *Network Newsletter* no. 21, British Council, November 2000

Analysing gender relations

If effective policy and practice responses to gender inequality are to be forged, it is essential to take into account the emergence of critical theory in relation to men and masculinities outlined above. In turn, this implies the need to develop sensitive gender analysis in order to assist the design, targeting, and implementation of interventions.

Various gender analysis frameworks exist which can be used to examine change towards gender equality; each proposes different critical dimensions of change and different indicators.[46] Oxfam's preferred approach draws in particular upon Kabeer's framework for gender and development planning,[47] which understands gender as one of a number of 'social relations' (the various structural relationships which create and maintain differences in the positioning of groups of people in society, such as age, race, class, ethnicity, disability, and sexual orientation).

According to this model, the underlying causes of gender inequality are produced and reinforced within four key institutional locations: the State, the market, the community, and the family or household. To address poverty and inequality it is important to examine in detail the values and practices within these institutions – and the links between the institutions – in order to understand who does what, who gains, and who loses.

Box 2: The 'Social Relations' approach

This approach classifies institutional gender policies into two basic types:

gender-blind policies, which fail to make any distinction between the sexes, and thereby entrench existing biases (often implicitly in favour of men);

gender-aware policies, which recognise that men and women have differing and sometimes conflicting needs, interests, and priorities. Gender-aware policies can also be further divided into:

- gender-neutral policies: interventions that target and benefit both sexes effectively, but leave the existing distribution of resources and responsibilities intact;
- gender-specific policies: interventions intended to meet the targeted needs of women or men, but which leave the existing distribution of resources and responsibilities intact;
- gender-redistributive policies: interventions intended to transform the existing distribution of resources and responsibilities to create a more balanced relationship between men and women.

Although it provides a relatively complex template, the 'Social Relations' approach is useful for many purposes, including project planning and policy development. For the current research, the tools of this framework are useful. While the limited scope and duration of this research means that the framework cannot be applied in its entirety, the approach provides a clear set of key concepts, which are relevant to work with men in developing countries and in the UK.

Summary

Rising suicides among young men; educational underachievement among boys; male detachment from the labour market: in the UK statistics such as these are regularly used to support the argument that masculinity is 'in crisis'. But the overall trends still show that women are the majority of those living in poverty in the UK. Moreover, in general men have the structural advantage of setting 'the norm'; most interventions and institutions are shaped around their interests. While talk of a male crisis may therefore be overdone, there are nevertheless real concerns regarding the position of some groups of men in the UK, especially those who are unemployed or economically inactive. The statistics show, for instance, that men living in the most economically deprived areas have far higher than average rates of mortality.

In recent years, new social research has increasingly recognised that there is no one universal pattern of masculinity (hence the use of 'masculinities'), and that significant cross-cutting issues such as class, race, age, disability, and sexual orientation must be taken into account too. Furthermore, 'collective' masculinities can operate beyond the individual, within culture and institutions. Masculinities are also actively 'produced' by individuals, rather than being programmed by genes or fixed by social structures. Finally, masculinities are dynamic, changing according to specific historical circumstances.

Various frameworks have been developed to undertake gender analysis. Oxfam favours that of Kabeer, who suggests the basic approaches of institutions (the State, the market, the community, and the family or household) can be classified as 'gender-blind' or 'gender-aware', categorisations which are used within the present research. Oxfam believes that undertaking such gender analysis is central to identifying and challenging the basic inequalities between men and women, and between particular groups of men and women.

3
Methodology

The main techniques used for this research were the collection and study of literature sources, and the gathering and analysis of primary interview data. Consultation was also undertaken on the project's draft findings with those who had participated in the research.

Literature review

Initially, a review of the existing literature on gender and poverty in the UK was undertaken. The developing pool of theoretical work on men and masculinities was also consulted to ensure that current critical perspectives were fully integrated into the project.

While there is a large body of analysis of poverty and social exclusion in the UK, work that focuses in particular on men as a target group is rare. However there have been some notable attempts to explore the impact of changing economic and social conditions on men.[1]

Research on working with men was then considered, in order to highlight key contextual issues and any mapping of services relevant to men in poverty. Research was sought which primarily addressed the UK, and another key source was Oxfam's existing publications on gender and development issues.[2]

Finally, the review explored more practice-orientated materials, drawing in particular on a wide range of articles in the British journal *Working With Men*, which has provided a key forum for professionals over the past decade.[3]

Primary research

Following the review, interviews with individuals or organisations working with men at the grassroots level were undertaken between

November 2000 and January 2001 in England and Wales by Sandy Ruxton (principal researcher), and in Scotland by Jill Mawson (research assistant). A defined set of questions was identified; interviews were semi-structured, however, in order to allow interviewees to raise the key concerns as they saw them.

Overall, representatives of 22 organisations were contacted in England and Wales, and a further six in Scotland, either by 'phone or face-to-face. A full list of these organisations is set out in the Appendix. It should be noted that in order to supplement the information derived from primary research, some project descriptions cited in the text were derived purely from published sources (such as websites).

Given that women represent the majority in the poorest groups in the UK, few if any projects appear to be established with the direct objective of tackling male poverty. The researchers therefore targeted organisations and individuals providing services in particular sectors for the purpose of the research. Employment and training, men's health, violence, and fatherhood were identified as the main themes to explore, chosen primarily on the basis that these services were likely to come into contact with significant numbers of men. The vast majority of projects working in these areas recognised that their work had an indirect impact on tackling poverty, even though this was not the initial motivation for their work.

Projects were selected to represent a diverse spread of work with men in the categories already outlined. The researchers also attempted to contact projects spanning the range from 'gender-blind' to 'gender-aware' (see Chapter 2). On the whole, projects with an apparent gender-awareness (as evidenced by published materials and articles, and the advice of respondents with an overview of particular sectors) were prioritised over the gender-blind, as the former were felt to be able to offer more insights to feed into the report's overall analysis.

Projects were also contacted across the UK to ensure that different regional and national perspectives could be taken into account. Project visits were undertaken in areas experiencing high levels of poverty, including Merthyr Tydfil in south Wales, Manchester and Salford in the north-west, and Glasgow in Scotland. In this way the research sought to highlight the different contexts within which masculinities are 'lived' in the UK, and the importance of solutions appropriate to national and local conditions.

Consultation phase

Once project interviews were completed, discussion of the initial findings was undertaken with a smaller number of individuals and organisations with more of an overview of specific areas of work, or a particular expertise in relation to the wider policy or political context. This was intended to test the applicability and relevance of the findings, and to help with developing a set of recommendations.

Following the writing of a draft report, a workshop was held in Oxford in March 2001 to share the interim conclusions, to explore issues in more detail, to obtain feedback, and to explore potential ways forward. Presentations were given by the report's author and by Peter Moss, Thomas Coram Research Unit (on gender and caring); Dave Morran, Stirling University (on work with men who use violence); Peter Baker, Men's Health Forum; and Sue Yeandle, Sheffield Hallam University (on economic inactivity and male employment).

Following the workshop, a further round of written consultation was undertaken by e-mail with the majority of those who had been interviewed, in order to check quotes and project details, and to flesh out aspects of the analysis. Final amendments were then made to the report prior to publication.

Reflections on the methodology

Three main methodological difficulties were encountered during the project. Firstly, the relatively unsophisticated approach to gender analysis among many projects and interviewees made it hard to apply the 'social relations' framework in full as a means of analysing gender relations. Although this is clearly a useful framework, it is relatively complex and arguably needs some refinement if it is to be easily applicable to the UK context. Having said this, Oxfam's experience of seeking to apply gender analysis internationally is instructive for a UK audience, where such an approach remains relatively unusual.

Second, the relatively small sample size for project interviews reinforces the importance of regarding the conclusions as tentative. Nevertheless, the cross-checking with existing literature, the discussion at the workshop, and the second round of written consultation on drafts of the report, have tended to confirm the validity and applicability of the findings.

Third, it may be suggested that drawing conclusions from brief project visits or telephone interviews is a hazardous endeavour. However in practice, the researchers often had access to additional written materials about the project, in the form of articles, annual reports, or presentations. Their assessments were therefore derived not only from their own application of the framework set out in Chapter 2, but also from careful consideration of what project members said or wrote about their own work.

4
Masculinities in the UK: the policy context

While the bulk of this study explores the perspectives of projects working at grassroots level, it is important to locate this experience within the overall policy context. This section therefore explores briefly the recent development of government policy to tackle poverty and social exclusion; the differential impact of such policy on men and women (especially on those in the most disadvantaged groups); and the existing institutional mechanisms for promoting gender equality.

The gender impact of government policies to tackle poverty and social exclusion

Gender impact assessment challenges the assumption that policies, programmes and legislation affect everyone in the same way. It puts people at the heart of policy-making and leads to better government by making gender equality visible in the mainstream of society. It sends the message that women and men are valued equally both for their similarities and differences and the varying roles they play.

Women and Equality Unit, 'Gender Impact Assessment: A Framework for Gender Mainstreaming', www.womenandequalityunit.gov.uk

Since coming to power in May 1997, the Labour government has made considerable progress in tackling poverty and social exclusion (although the differential impact on men and women is as yet unclear). Official figures[1] highlight the fact that the number of people living in households with less than 60 per cent of median income after housing costs was 12.9 million in 2000-2001, one million less than in 1996-1997. This is a significant improvement, given the doubling of these figures during the 1980s.[2] Unemployment is at its lowest levels since the 1970s, and long-term youth unemployment has been virtually eradicated. In relation to the goal of ending child poverty in 20 years, announced by the Prime Minister in 1997, around half a million children have been lifted out of poverty; less than originally claimed, but progress nonetheless.[3]

The government is tackling poverty and social exclusion through a range of policies and programmes. These include:

- real improvements in benefit levels, especially for younger children, pensioners, carers on income support, and severely disabled people (although there were also cuts for lone parents, and some disabled people will lose out from benefit changes);
- a pledge to eradicate child poverty in two decades, together with a package of measures to benefit children (for example, a real increase in child benefit, the Working Families Tax Credit, and the Sure Start programme);[4]
- the introduction of a basic minimum wage;
- an embryonic National Childcare Strategy (although the supply of places remains insufficient), and some family-friendly employment measures (e.g. parental leave, paid paternity leave, improvements to maternity pay);
- other employment rights (such as regulations on working time, new rights for part-time and fixed-term workers), partly prompted by EU directives;
- the flagship New Deal programmes[5] to tackle unemployment and worklessness by improving work and training opportunities;
- area-based initiatives (for example, Action Zones in relation to employment, health, and education);
- the establishment of the Social Exclusion Unit, which has developed policies on a number of specific problems including that of rough sleeping, together with an ambitious national strategy for neighbourhood renewal.

Despite the impact of these measures, critics argue that the government has failed to tackle the deep-seated structural inequalities that underlie the growth in poverty and social exclusion. Although some limited 'redistribution by stealth' has taken place since the current government came to power, income inequality rose marginally overall in the late 90s, as benefits fell behind the rise in real incomes for some.[6] It has been suggested that the government's failure to champion openly any form of redistribution makes any possible future commitment to such an agenda more vulnerable. But the 2002 Budget may herald a new approach to taxation, by putting an extra one per cent on national insurance contributions in order to fund a massive rise in UK health-spending from 6.7 per cent of GDP in 1997 to 9.4 per cent by 2007-2008.[7]

A range of organisations including the Fabian Society, the New Policy Institute, and Oxfam GB, has also suggested that a truly national strategy against poverty and social exclusion must involve stakeholders beyond the UK government itself: including the private and voluntary sectors, trade unions, local government, and people with direct experience of poverty and social exclusion.[8] This is a very different emphasis from the approach of the current government hitherto, which has focused on projects and initiatives that are administered and paid for by central government itself.

How far the government's strategy on poverty and social exclusion has been shaped by an understanding of the differing needs and interests of poor men and women is less easy to define. Critics argue that progress in gender assessment has been slow, and that too often a whole-family perspective is still used in policy-making, obscuring the impact on men and women. Nevertheless, analysis apparently being undertaken by the Treasury (based on certain assumptions about how finance is split within households) appears to suggest that tax and benefit policies such as those outlined above – and especially measures focused on children and pensioners, and income tax changes – have significantly improved women's access to income and other resources relative to men over the lifetime of the last parliament.[9] Men have apparently gained more recently, however, from such initiatives as the introduction of the children's tax credit, in spite of having tended to lose out as a result of changes in the earlier years of the Labour government (for example, from the abolition of MIRAS tax relief and the married couple's allowance).[10]

In relation to employment policy, a report on the UK for the European Commission's Expert Group on Gender and Employment[11] recently concluded that the available studies by government bodies 'tend to lack any real analysis of gender'. Moreover, even where important gender differences are revealed, these findings 'are not integrated into government thinking and policy analysis'. For example, a report by the Low Pay Commission[12] has shown that two-thirds of the beneficiaries of the minimum wage have been women, and that two-thirds of these have been in part-time work. Recent research also indicates, however, that

... policy-makers are too wary of looking inside the 'black box' of the couple as a unit in order to examine transfers of resources and relationships, or who receives income and in what form, and to what use it is put, as well as how much it is.

Women's Budget Group, Pre-Budget Report Response, November 2001, www.wbg.org.uk

there is little evidence of any substantial decline in the overall gender pay gap as a result of the national minimum wage, largely because it has been set at too low a level.[13] It remains to be seen what the effect will be of additional increases to be introduced in October 2002.[14]

The thrust of the government's welfare reforms to tackle poverty and social exclusion has concentrated not only on 'making work pay', but also on 'welfare to work'. It has been suggested that this approach in practice has afforded low priority to gender equality (rather than the reduction of 'workless' households or child poverty).[15] For instance, the Working Families Tax Credit tends to emphasise the importance of getting one person within a household into work, rather than ensuring the economic independence of both male and female family members. The resulting impact of the emphasis on paid employment may also be to devalue forms of unpaid work, notably domestic care and community and voluntary work (much of which is currently undertaken by women).

In addition, more than half of the spending on the £2.6 billion New Deal programme (57 per cent) goes to the New Deal for Young People, and a further 23 per cent to the New Deal for the Long-term Unemployed. Men make up over 70 per cent of entrants to the former, and 84 per cent to the latter. There is a trade-off: although the greater proportion of overall resources are therefore spent on men, these two programmes entail a far greater degree of compulsory participation than the New Deal for Lone Parents and the New Deal for Partners, which are mainly taken up by women.

The brief summary of the areas identified above suggests that a relatively gender-blind approach to the potential impact on men and women tended to predominate within Labour government policy until recently. Indeed, the fact that any serious attempts to undertake gender impact assessment are only now getting under way reinforces the view that until relatively recently policy has been developed – and sold politically – based on existing assumptions rather than an analysis of impact.

Having said this, the seeds of a more gender-aware approach are also discernible, particularly in policy areas addressed in more detail in the main bulk of this report (and also in relation to some issues not covered here, such as boys' education). The fact that initiatives to tackle men's violence, improve men's health, and encourage responsible fatherhood have been instigated is evidence that men's distinct needs and interests are being addressed to some extent.

Institutional mechanisms for promoting gender equality

It would be wrong to identify either males or females as being more in need of attention from policy-makers. Both genders have areas of their lives in which they may be at risk, and a key task is to clarify the differing needs of females and males so that these risk factors can be addressed.

C. Dennison, J. Coleman, *Young People and Gender: A Review of Research*, Women's Unit and the Family Policy Unit, 2000

Attempts to ensure that gender is mainstreamed[16] across all policy areas depend to a significant degree on the effectiveness of the institutional mechanisms to promote such an approach. When first elected, the Labour government set up new structures within Whitehall to underpin a greater emphasis on gender equality; however, it appears that innovations at devolved level have had greater impact in practice.

At UK level, the Women's Unit (together with a Minister for Women in the Cabinet and a second Minister in support) was first established in the Department of Social Security in 1997, and then moved to the Cabinet Office in 1998. In 2001 the Unit was again shifted, this time to the Department for Trade and Industry, and re-titled the 'Women and Equality Unit'. Initially the role of the Unit was to advise on initiatives, consider policies across government, and support the development of joined-up thinking. In practice, however, the Unit has not been well integrated into policy-making, and has tended to remain in a peripheral location within governmental structures (even when in the Cabinet Office). In contrast to the Social Exclusion Unit, it has also been poorly aligned with many of the government's public programmes.[17] The prospects for the Unit to make an impact, however, seem better than in the government's first term. Following the 2001 election, the Unit's remit was widened to include other equality issues (including age, sexual orientation, and religion) as well as gender, and its budget was doubled between 1998-1999 and 2001-2002.[18]

The challenge of mainstreaming gender into the policy-making process remains a significant one, and gender impact assessment is still not systematically applied across departments. Although guidelines for equal treatment for race, sex, and disability were published jointly in 1998 by the then Women's Unit, Department for Education and Employment, and Home Office, they are too limited to promote proactive equality policies.[19] Moreover, they have not been universally applied by all departments, and the only department to have developed a clear and consistent gender perspective in its work is the Department for International Development. More recently, the Women and Equality Unit has been overseeing the piloting by several departments of more robust gender impact assessments for certain policies. In contrast to the Policy Appraisal for Equal Treatment Guidelines,[20] the pilot assessments are more wide-ranging and ambitious, moving beyond a basic analysis of whether existing policies are lawful and justifiable.

Progress under devolution has tended to be swifter. In Wales, for example, the National Assembly is under a broad-ranging statutory duty to promote equality. Flowing from this overall commitment, a distinctive equality agenda has started to emerge, with reforms being initiated in most areas of the legislature's functioning. One initial assessment has concluded that 'equality of opportunity is beginning to be addressed in a systematic way at an all-Wales level of government for the first time'. Reflecting UK-wide developments, an Equality Policy Unit was set up to support this programme.[21]

In Scotland, all Executive Bills have to be accompanied by a statement of their likely impact on equal opportunities, and a mainstreaming checklist has been developed for Members of the Scottish Parliament. An Equality Unit was also established in 1999.[22] Under the 1998 Northern Ireland Act, public authorities are required to have due regard to the need to promote equality of opportunity, with the recently established Equality Commission responsible for overseeing implementation.

Summary

The government has made some progress in tackling poverty and social exclusion through a range of policies and programmes, which include improvements in benefit levels for some groups, a package of child-focused measures, introduction of a basic minimum wage, the New Deal, and establishment of the Social Exclusion Unit.

As a result of a lack of both gender-disaggregated statistics on which to base effective policy[23] and the political will to provide momentum, there is as yet insufficient evidence to identify in any detail the differential impact of these policies on men and women (and on particular groups of men and women). Based on the information which is available, a tentative assessment suggests that women may have benefited more from direct redistribution, while greater resources have been spent on developing men's human capital.

Overall, it appears that the initiatives taken and the mechanisms established by the government, welcome though they are, have as yet been insufficient to develop and sustain coherent gender mainstreaming across all policy areas. Expansion of the role and resources of the original Women's Unit following the 2001 election, however, may be indicative of an increased commitment on the part of government. Similar moves towards gender impact assessment have advanced more quickly at devolved levels. It is to be hoped that the growing focus on 'gender' and 'equality' together may herald a more integrated agenda, and that within this, issues of men and masculinities can be addressed in a way which goes beyond simply shoring up the traditional socio-economic bases of male power.

5
Employment and training: making masculinities visible

The government has made raising employment levels the centrepiece of its anti-poverty strategy. In 1999, the Treasury argued in an important paper that 'work is the most important route to increased prosperity, and most people who are trapped on low income are without work'.[1] This approach underpins the government's welfare reform strategy of 'work for those who can, security for those who cannot', made up largely of 'welfare to work' initiatives (including the New Deal), and attempts to make work pay through tax and national insurance reforms.

Promoting paid work as the main route out of poverty is widely supported, both in the UK and at European level.[2] Critics have suggested, however, that paid work is not an automatic passport to social inclusion. There is also some resentment that other forms of work, notably community or voluntary and domestic care work – mostly being undertaken by women – are being undervalued.[3]

Given the continuing centrality of the 'breadwinner' ethic to the self-image of many men, any attempt to analyse the nature, scope, and effectiveness of work with men which targets poverty (directly or indirectly) must explore the impact of the government's efforts to boost employment and training. This section therefore highlights key aspects of the changing labour market and their consequences for men on low incomes; analyses how far current employment training provision is gender-aware in its approach; explores how the needs of men in different age groups can best be met; and identifies some appropriate ways forward.

The impact of the changing labour market

Women remain disadvantaged overall in the UK labour market compared with men (see Chapter 2), but the position of men who have become detached from employment has worsened. In comparison, for those in work, the position appears to have improved owing to factors such as the introduction of the minimum wage and work-related tax credits, and registered unemployment fell between 1996 and 2001.

Since the 1980s, one of the most significant changes in the labour market has been the large rise in the number of men of working age (especially older men) who have become 'economically inactive' (that is, not employed or recorded as being unemployed). While these official figures fail to acknowledge unpaid work,[4] the transformation in the position of men within them is nevertheless striking.

According to research by Fothergill, *et al.*,[5] at the end of the 1990s the group of inactive men outnumbered the recorded unemployed by more than two-to-one. Among the 'economically inactive' counted in official statistics, men defined as 'long-term sick' or 'disabled' are the biggest single group, forming 25 per cent of the three million economically inactive men.[6] A number of factors appear to have influenced this trend, including government encouragement (especially in the 1980s) for claimants to move off the unemployment register and onto disability and sickness benefits, and tighter approaches to staff selection among employers.[7] It may also be the case that some men retreat from increasingly difficult circumstances into incapacity. The main findings of the research by Fothergill *et al.* also revealed further disturbing information about the experience of economically inactive and long-term unemployed men in areas of greatest decline. For example:

- Such men are found in large numbers in traditional industrial areas affected by job losses such as south Wales, north-east England, Merseyside, Clydeside and South Yorkshire, where they represent up to 30 per cent of the entire population of 25-64 year-old men.
- Apart from part-time workers, the main groups of men in this age group who are detached from full-time employment are (in descending order of size) the long-term sick or disabled, the long-term unemployed, the early retired, and full-time carers. Of these categories, 98 per cent of the long-term sick or disabled were benefit claimants, Incapacity Benefit being the main form of support.
- Among older and some younger men, chronic ill-health and disability are widespread, some of it attributable to unhealthy and unsafe environments in previous employment.

- Most inactive men find coping on an out-of-work income very difficult, and is not a situation of choice, except for some of the early-retired.

Particular attention has also focused on the needs of young men, especially because of fears that unemployment among this group has led to a rise in family breakdown, anti-social behaviour, and even the emergence of a so-called 'underclass'. Research by the Centre for Research in Social Policy[8] has found that young men's underachievement is possibly less severe than some had feared; nevertheless, the economic position of young men has deteriorated over time. And although more young men have stayed on in education, later generations of young men are more likely to enter the labour market as unemployed and have a greater chance of being unemployed subsequently.

Based on existing trends, the job prospects for young men from ethnic minorities are especially bleak. For example, a study by Berthoud[9] found that young Caribbean men are more than twice as likely to be unemployed as young white men, and they also have lower earnings. On average, the circumstances of Pakistani and Bangladeshi men are worse still, as they are more likely to be unemployed than Caribbean men.

> One of the most pronounced changes in the UK labour market over the last two decades has been the rise in the number of economically inactive men of working age. These are men aged between 16 and 64 who are neither employed nor recorded as unemployed ... In spring 2000, 3.0 million men were economically inactive, or 16 per cent of the male working age population.
>
> National Statistics, *Social Focus on Men*, The Stationery Office, 2001

The picture above is illustrated by the views expressed by men and women during a gender needs assessment conducted in 1999 by the Gellideg Foundation (a small locally-run community group on a housing estate in Merthyr Tydfil in south Wales) with the assistance of Oxfam's UK Poverty Programme. The assessment, derived from 73 interviews with local residents, highlighted a range of barriers facing marginalised men and women in the area: personal (including training and education levels, ill health, and lack of confidence and self-esteem); social (including ideas and beliefs); and structural (including barriers within the labour market, the benefits system, and local services and facilities).

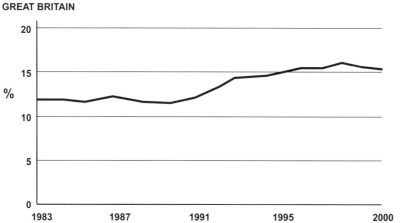

Figure 3:
Economic inactivity rates among men*

*Men aged 16 to 64.
Rates at spring each year.

*Source: Labour Force Survey,
Office for National Statistics*

Gellideg Gender Needs Assessment

- Men, unlike women, have a good overview of the local job market, and assess it from what they feel is their job of bringing home enough wages to provide long term security. The bare minimum money from employment does not encourage them into work.

- Men are very aware of the shortcomings of the benefits system to meet short and long-term needs. Men see benefits as very basic, not enough to meet immediate needs, and not meeting needs in times of crisis. They cannot provide for a comfortable retirement, or contribute to savings. Moving from benefits to employment is hard – there is no hope of starting a business with no capital, and when benefits stop, you struggle for finances as there is no back up and no leeway from the government – rent starts straightaway, and when work starts there is no pay in hand.

- Men are very clear that any training they might do would have to be work-related. They fear that sickness benefit will stop if they want to take up training opportunities. They feel there is a need for more money when in training. Men do not feel employable after the age of 40 and feel there is no point in taking up training or education as they will not get a job anyway. They recognize that competition for jobs means the computer-literate young get the chances, although as older workers they have plenty of experience in both formal and informal employment.

Gellideg Foundation and Oxfam GB, extracts from 'Gender in Gellideg: Survival strategies on a housing estate in south Wales', 2001

Employment training: the gender-blind approach

Compared with other schemes researched during the course of this study, employment projects tended towards a more gender-blind approach. As Trefor Lloyd of Working With Men put it: 'They tend to treat men as a fact rather than a factor in their work.'

This was confirmed by Robert Cornwall of the Gurnos Centre,[10] a New Deal provider in Merthyr Tydfil in the south Wales valleys. He argued that the New Deal tended to be designed with men as the norm, and that the centre currently does little to address gender issues. In practice, it is heavily male-dominated: all the four tutors are male, and the number of women attending is very small. In Cornwall's view, this imbalance appears to be largely justifiable. This is based on his assessment that it is primarily men who are disadvantaged in the local labour market, given the new type of work available, and the higher levels of male as opposed to female 'economic inactivity' (particularly due to illness) in the valleys.[11]

Discussions with others confirmed to the researcher that 'gender-blindness' was a common problem among employment and training providers. It appears that there are several reasons for this. Firstly, the generic training modules provided by government and others do not tend to focus on the impact of gender (as a DfEE researcher indicated to us). Second, programme targets are not set to reflect gender as an issue, and consequently (within the context of a traditional area in particular), there is no incentive to alter established training patterns. Third, programmes are increasingly being designed to meet the explicit recruitment needs and practices of employers; therefore if employers do not recognise the importance of gender issues, these will not be addressed by programmes.

Finally, labour market programmes have often been, in Cornwall's words, 'designed in Sheffield, and applied locally'. As a result they have not been developed with sufficient sensitivity to local conditions. In the case of the Gurnos Centre, the closure of coal mines in the area during the 1980s has had a profound and lasting impact on the economic and social environment. Many men still draw upon long-standing traditional patriarchal structures and attitudes, regarding themselves primarily as breadwinners yet unwilling or unable to adapt to the changing labour market. As a result the main topics that are taught – construction, carpentry, and interior decoration – tend to reflect traditional stereotypes rather than the needs of local labour markets.

A similar picture is found in other parts of the country, particularly the north-east of England, where an area with an economy historically based on heavy industry has suffered serious decline, to the extent that there is now only one working coal mine in the region, steel production has terminated, and ship-building survives with difficulty. This has had a significant impact on families and communities. As a report from Newcastle-based group Fathers Plus describes the situation:

> For unskilled or semi-skilled people, the outlook is bleak and unemployment rates, though improving, are still significantly higher than the rest of the country. A number of local and central govern-ment initiatives have been successful in encouraging new industrial and commercial development in the area, but these have often been seen as better suited to women in terms of skills required, the shifts offered and part-time work available. Although re-training is offered as men generally lack the skills demanded by the new opportunities, the take-up has tended to be slow, as people take time to come to terms with new constraints and challenges and what they perceive this to mean for their identity as breadwinner.[12]

Meeting the needs of younger men

Boys who fail at school fail to find jobs and become increasingly marginalised. Status zero is the sociological term used to describe the increasing numbers of young people – mainly boys – who have effectively ceased to be part of mainstream society. To regenerate our communi-ties, we must begin to tackle the disaffection of young men and boys ...

The changes in our society are here to stay. Too many boys are failing to adapt to them. They need to be more aware of the implications of a changing labour market and changing family patterns. They need to be better equipped to respond constructively to the challenges they face, and to maintain a greater commitment to learning as a life-long process. Too many boys are succumbing to the notion that there is no point in learning – to a group culture where it is 'cool' to truant, and to indulge in anti-social behaviour.

Estelle Morris, MP, 'Boys will be boys; (Closing the gender gap)', consultation paper, Labour Party, 1996

A gender-aware approach needs to take into account not only the often hidden needs of women in relation to training and employment, but also the significance of masculinity issues and the variations between different groups of men.

In reality, most employment training is directed at young men by default. This focus is to some extent understandable given the risks (such as offending, heavy drinking, and drug usage) associated with some groups of young men who fail to enter the labour market, or exit from it at an early stage.[13] The barriers to young men taking up employment are often summarised as lack of skills and work experience, ineffective job-seeking, low pay, and access to and costs of transport.[14]

Our research tends to confirm that these factors are highly relevant, but in addition it suggests that underpinning all these issues is the centrality of dominant notions of masculinity for young men (particularly working class men). Carrying with them a legacy of underachievement and rebellion in school, many young men, especially in areas experiencing the sharp end of labour-market change, appear to believe that it is simply not 'macho' to go into training. As there is no forum for any deeper discussion around what it is to be a man today, and new roles and expectations, many young men enter and leave courses with the same expectations and misconceptions. It seems likely that the failure of employment training to engage with their agenda in any coherent way is a significant factor in the high drop-out rates.

> Beliefs about men's role and masculinity are important components within the career decision-making process. None of the young men indicated any opportunities to reflect on these processes and attitudes, while there were suggestions that adults had actively discouraged them from making what were seen as inappropriate 'unmanly' decisions.
>
> T. Lloyd, *Young Men's Attitudes to Gender and Work*, Joseph Rowntree Foundation, 1999

Research by Lloyd[15] confirmed the entrenched nature of young men's attitudes towards the labour market. In his study, most said they were poorly prepared at school for the workplace. Careers advice, family involvement, and even work experience had been of limited value, and combined with a reluctance on their part to accept any advice given. All the men interviewed also made a distinction between 'crap jobs' and 'career' jobs, viewing the former as temporary and primarily a source of money.

A particularly salient factor in Lloyd's research was the finding that although the majority made few distinctions between jobs for men and jobs for women, in practice they ruled out certain jobs on the basis of the pay and skills involved. Many of these jobs would typically be done by women, suggesting that young men's choices draw upon long-standing perceptions that have consistently devalued the real level of skill of 'women's work' (both reproductive work and work for pay). Within the context of the changing labour market, where interpersonal and communication skills and high standards of customer service (skills more traditionally associated with women) are frequently at a premium, it seems likely that marginalised young men's expectations in terms of status and pay will increasingly not be met.[16]

In these circumstances there is an argument that all the key agencies involved – schools, careers services, and employers – need to pay greater attention to promoting gender equality in career choices. There is also a need to develop policies to improve terms and conditions (particularly within the service sector). This straightforward conclusion is supported by research published by the Equal Opportunities Commission in 1999, which found that only a third of Careers Services had most of the features required of a sound equal opportunities policy, including an agenda for policy and practice and a structure for implementation.[17] Moreover, only four Careers Services had an agenda for positive action to address gender stereotyping and segregated choices.

It is unclear how far the Connexions Service (the new youth support service for 13 to 19 year olds in England), will be successful in building equality into careers education and guidance. Its focus on those most at risk of underachievement or disaffection, together with a personal adviser system, is likely to prove valuable, however. It is also important to acknowledge that additional forms of intervention may be necessary to improve the links between education and labour market institutions. As McDowell suggests:

> It may be that local connections between particular schools and
> relatively local employers might be forged. In some cities in the
> United States, for example, local employers, including hotel and
> restaurant chains and large retailers, have developed educational
> programmes in conjunction with schools in deprived areas with
> high rates of post-school unemployment, guaranteeing jobs to
> school leavers subject to certain levels of attainment and a satisfactory
> personal report.[18]

Working With Men

37

Working With Men's 'Into Work' programme for boys and young men

Drawing upon initial research conducted by Lloyd, described above, the 'Into Work' programme aims to:

- develop approaches that would impact on socially excluded young men in their preparation for the workplace;
- develop and publish resource materials for teachers and careers officers to use in their work with young men;
- produce guidelines for schools for appropriate careers advice to socially excluded young men;
- identify individual needs and additional help for groups of young men;
- develop criteria for identifying young men who would benefit from a more extended careers curriculum.

To date, five programmes have been delivered in south London schools to 48 young men (aged 14-15). The programmes have included:

- seven school-based sessions on extensive interview experience; phone experience; help in the completion of application forms; advice about training options after school; experience of where and how to look for jobs; information about the changing workforce and workplace (including gender issues); opportunities to discuss personal career options, and
- six workplace visits, including three half-days arranged by the young men themselves to workplaces of their choice, and visits to a college, job centre, and careers office.

Feedback from participants indicates that the course helped them to increase their understanding and knowledge ('I now know how a college works'), to identify a career path and be focused ('It made me go for the right thing'), to raise their confidence ('It taught me not to be afraid to get some help'), and to identify barriers they will need to overcome ('I have to work harder'). Lloyd concludes that there were three main factors that contributed to success:

> The relevance of the topic. We talked to them about being men, and related to them as individuals with aspirations and expected them to behave accordingly. We never forgot that they were

individuals. Young men of 14-16 have often told us that too many teachers treat them the same as they did when they were eleven and that they were treated as part of a pack and not as individuals.

The materials, while not being wildly radical, were relevant and usually used for discussion starters. What was radical was the practical nature of the whole course. Instead of talking about the workplace, the young men went out to it. Instead of talking about interviewing and what employers were looking for, we interviewed them.

T. Lloyd, 'Boys and young men "Into Work" programme', *Working With Young Men*, Volume 1, January 2002

The LEAP Project

LEAP was set up to work with unemployed people in north London in Harlesden, south Kilburn, and Queen's Park in 1996, and aims to relieve poverty and distress through the provision of advice, information, training, and education. The project works primarily with black and ethnic minority young people, although other age groups are represented too.

Prospective clients first have an informal discussion with an adviser, to explore how they can best be helped. Most are invited back to attend the STRIVE workshop that is run each month, and which is based on a rigorous programme that has been used successfully to support disadvantaged young black people in Harlem in New York, and has spread across the USA.

The LEAP programme is an intensive job-readiness programme that focuses on the essential skills that are needed to succeed in the world of work. Once they have completed a three-week training programme, each client is assigned to a Placement Officer, who provides them with one-to-one support and guidance in their attempts to secure employment. Clients have access to a job-search room, which has newspapers with recruitment advertisements; computers on which they can do typing tests, design CV's, and write covering letters; telephones to contact potential employers or training courses; and the Adult Directions database. At any time during this process, if either the client or the Placement Officer identifies the need or desire for more specific or specialist training provision, they will be referred accordingly. Follow-up work and further support is provided for at least two years after a client first secures employment, to help with any problems in adjusting to the workplace environment, or to help them find another job, if necessary. LEAP has placed over 2,500 people into employment to date, and around 70 per cent of course attendees find jobs.

Especially important is the project's sensitivity to the particular difficulties facing young black men. For example, chief executive Tunde Banjuko points out that young black men often '... don't look people in the eye. That is perceived by employers as a sign of the black male being "shifty" or "untrustworthy", but in black and Asian culture it is seen as bad manners to look your father in the eye. So what is actually happening is the person is exhibiting deference, but that is being misinterpreted and ends up with the person not getting the job.'

Based on information from the LEAP website, www.leap.org.uk

'Older men don't make a fuss'

Despite the assumption implicit in many programmes for long-term unemployed people, unemployment is not just a consequence of lack of basic or specific skills and a lack of 'flexibility' on the part of individuals. It is also the consequence of changing global and domestic markets, domestic economic policies, industrial and organisational restructuring and rampant ageism in the labour market. Often it is the result of ill health and disability. Many unemployed men are highly trained, skilled and experienced workers who are not to blame for the restructuring, downsizing or overall scaling-down of industries that have destroyed their jobs. The implication that they are not sufficiently 'employable' can be insulting.

V. McGivney, 'Excluded Men: Men who are missing from education and training', NIACE, 1999

Despite the range of serious issues facing older working class men outlined in the research of Fothergill *et al.* above, there has been little attempt to address the employment and training needs of this group (although the relatively recent introduction nationwide of New Deal 50plus[19] in April 2000 has begun to redress this balance). As Colette Carol of CREST, a project in Salford providing a drop-in centre and IT facilities which is currently supported by Oxfam's UK Poverty Programme, put it to us: 'older men don't make a fuss, and their needs therefore get ignored'. This is in spite of the existence of the New Deal for the Long-Term Unemployed programme (targeted at those aged 25 plus who have been unemployed for 12, 18, or 24 months, depending on area), the vast proportion of whose client group are men. As an evaluation for the Employment Service has shown, NDLTU has failed to establish the same support and shared aims as other New Deal programmes:

> For some long-term unemployed adults the (NDLTU) programme has been a helpful intervention with positive outcomes. This was especially true of those who had low expectations of the programme on entry but who had been re-motivated and supported by the programme. Other more highly motivated clients appear to have been frustrated by NDLTU provision, or rather lack of it, while a body of unemployed people were deeply cynical about all government programmes and resented any compulsion to take part in NDLTU.
>
> C. Hasluck, 'Early Lessons from the Evaluation of New Deal Programmes', Employment Service, 2000

In general it has tended to be accepted that older working class men in particular are unwilling to enter training schemes. One key factor is that their self-image is closely connected to paid employment rather than training. Another is that they are apprehensive of involvement in education, and fear that more training could result in renewed failure. Some would argue that these elements may be present for younger men too. There is a strong case, however, that the experience of loss faced by older men who have been made redundant or have found their current skills and training less relevant in a changing labour market, is likely to be far more profound and debilitating.

An early evaluation of New Deal 50plus[20] suggests that around three-quarters of older men who have experienced the programme think that the advice and guidance they have received is useful (whether or not they have actually found work subsequently). Respondents are also largely very positive about the Employment Credit, which adds around £60 per week for full-time work, and view it as an incentive to find work, despite its one-year limit.

A number of barriers to employment remain for this group, including age discrimination among employers; the decline of certain industries; dependency on benefits and a fear of being financially worse off by working; health and disability issues; and transport and literacy problems.

The case of CREST highlights problems of isolation and low self-esteem for this group. Most of the men on the project are on Incapacity Benefit rather than Job Seekers Allowance, reflecting the findings of the Fothergill research. Many are on their own, tending to spend most of their time at home and hardly going out at all. As key community roles tend to be played more often by women, and working men's clubs have generally declined, they feel they have no community role.

In addition, according to CREST staff, older men are put under more pressure than women to attempt to get work, especially from job centres. This can be particularly hard for older male carers. Several of the men attending CREST are caring for elderly relatives, having been made redundant or given up their jobs voluntarily. The men get a carer's allowance, but this is cut when the relative dies, and they are then pursued by the Employment Service to get a job. Having in some cases reconstructed a new identity for themselves as carers and become detached from the labour market, their skills are out of date, their ability to function in a work context is poor, and they are incapable of planning ahead for their futures.

There is an argument that compulsion ensures that all eligible clients do receive the benefit of programmes, though others suggest that compulsion is counterproductive, producing a truculent workforce, higher drop-out rates, and inhibiting more constructive relationships with personal advisers. In general, it appears that among New Deal clients at least, compulsion for certain groups (young people and long-term unemployed, for example) is viewed more favourably than compulsion for others (such as older workers, lone parents, disabled people, and partners). One overview of recent New Deal evaluation studies confirmed the suggestion above that 'the difference seems to relate, at least in part, to the other roles and responsibilities of these groups, particularly caring roles.'[21]

Research by McGivney[22] highlighted a range of factors that help to improve the motivation and participation of men over 25. In relation to common difficulties in recruitment, she provides evidence that telephone help-lines, face-to-face guidance in familiar and informal settings, and outreach strategies to contact men through venues such as pubs and sports clubs can be effective. In addition, she suggests it is important to carry out research locally into why men do not participate in education and training. For some, it appears that peer-group approaches (through workplaces and community organisations, for example) can be more successful in drawing men in than individual approaches. Designing appropriate programmes for men is also key; for example, men are often more receptive to learning computer skills in single-sex groups, as they believe that women have better keyboard skills. Men usually participate in learning for practical and job-related reasons, so approaches must be developed which are relevant to their everyday life and concerns.

... among those men aged 25 and over leaving the New Deal programme in March 2001, a much lower proportion moved into employment – only 15 per cent compared with 40 per cent of 18-24 year olds.

National Statistics, *Social Focus on Men*, The Stationery Office, 2001

Towards gender-awareness in employment training?

If men, especially those who are unemployed, are to gain from learning opportunities, it is essential that efforts should be increased to tackle the factors that prevent them from doing so. One study concluded that:

... they are prevented from engaging in education by a combination of powerful deterrents: structural constraints and institutional rigidities; scepticism about the value of learning and strongly held views about what constitutes appropriate male behaviour.[23]

In part, addressing these issues depends on a cultural transformation of attitudes among men. While some do recast their identities, particularly in the face of economic change (for example by becoming carers), the majority remain wedded to traditional notions of masculinity and the breadwinner role. Readiness to participate in learning is therefore often inhibited by fixed views on male and female roles, and an assumption that learning ends on leaving school.

This task is not only one for projects and programmes to address; this study found that in general, most employment training is to a large extent gender-blind, failing to acknowledge the importance of tackling issues like these. This is not to say that it is impossible to do so, indeed targeted provision can be very effective. What is important is to ensure that programmes have practical outcomes for men, with clearly focused content and objectives involving 'doing' rather than just 'talking'. There is also an important role for information technology in attracting men to learning. Training should also be delivered in familiar venues, based on local partnerships.

There is some evidence that more sensitive approaches are emerging, if only on a small scale. This can be illustrated not only by the projects highlighted earlier in this chapter, but also by the examples of Let's Get Serious in Greater Manchester, and the Simon Community in Glasgow.

Let's Get Serious

Based in Old Trafford, Let's Get Serious was set up to target men's health needs as a priority (based partly on very poor health indicators and high suicide rates). It is a project based in the Manchester, Salford, and Trafford Health Action Zone, with three-year funding from the Innovation Fund.[24]

The project aims to provide a network of support for boys aged 8-16 who are in danger of becoming marginalised because of educational under-achievement, high drug use, and challenging behaviour. It employs a team of mentors, aged 16-40, who each support the emotional and educational development of several boys under 16. The mentors are drawn from men who have been unemployed for at least one year (identified through existing community groups), and the aim is to boost their skills, status, and self-image within the community. Most are working in placements in schools, although mentors have also worked with sports clubs, Social Services, and Millennium Awards Youth Offending Teams.

According to the project leader, Richard Strittmater, the experience of giving responsibility to mentors has been 'brilliant' and feedback from them has been extremely positive (as it has been from mentees). One reason for this is that mentors have received wide-ranging training and (controversially) are paid £15,000 a year. This is a higher than average salary for mentoring, but Strittmater feels it is necessary to pay at this level if they are to avoid alternative lifestyles (such as drugs use, crime, high-risk behaviour, or violence). The relatively high salary is also a strong incentive for the mentors to continue with the scheme, as they do not want to risk their new-found status and prosperity and slip back into poverty and social exclusion.

While there does not appear to be a comprehensive gender analysis behind this project, it is clearly attempting to respond positively to the difficulties facing long-term unemployed men in a disadvantaged area. An initial stakeholder survey suggested that there would be indirect benefits for women locally, and the staff indicate there is no overriding reason why complementary work could not be targeted directly at women in the future. In addition, the project is undertaking research on the huge cost to society of not doing work like this (in terms of the costs of probation, policing, welfare benefits, and vandalism). For example, it costs over £25,000 per annum to keep one person in prison, and double that to keep a young person in a young offenders' institution.[25]

Let's Get Serious gave 21-year-old Dean his first-ever job interview. Previously, Dean had been involved in voluntary work with the local drugs charity, Lifeline:

> *Somebody suggested I'd be good at this job because of my own experience of problems. That's made me feel a bit better about myself. My parents and friends are seeing a change in my attitude altogether. I feel like a different person. I feel better, more confident.*

> Dean

> *My problems started in primary school. I got expelled at the age of seven, though I was bright and had a lot of potential. It was due to lack of attention. I think guys crave attention, especially young boys. We were in the same situation as the kids we are going to help now. We've been there, in that scene. Maybe if I'd had a mentor when I was a young man I would have progressed better.*

> Adrian, trainee mentor

Based on a project visit and on material from the Health Development Agency website http://www.hda-online.org.uk/html/hdt0701/local3.html

---

The Simon Community

The Simon Community works with homeless people aged over 25, in Glasgow. Staff estimate that 85 per cent of those sleeping rough in the city are men, although in fact the project offers more beds to women than men. The lives of their clients have usually been chaotic and unsettled for some time, and they may have a history of alcohol or drug abuse, educational failure, criminality, and relationship difficulties. Thus the standard routes to structured training and employment are often unsuitable. Programmes such as New Deal are simply too different from a homeless person's 'norm' to be helpful.

The Simon Community therefore provides training under the 'New Futures Initiative' funded by the Scottish Executive, as the first stage towards possibly entering New Deal. Training focuses on the emotional and practical needs of individuals, and ranges from curtain making and photography to computer skills. Classes tend not to be split according to gender (although anger-management classes are for men only), and have been very effective in breaking down gender stereotypes. Despite the fact that traditional notions of masculinity among older men in Scotland appear enduring, the experience of the Simon Community of bringing a gender ethos to their work (if not a formal gender policy) has been positive.

Based on J. Mawson, unpublished report for Oxfam GB on Work with Men in Scotland, 2000

Working With Men

Summary

Although their position relative to women has declined, men as a group still fare better in the UK labour market. The circumstances of some men in work have also improved, owing to factors such as the introduction of the minimum wage (although in practice this has probably affected younger men more, many of whom are not family breadwinners). The evidence suggests, however, that in comparison with other men, the employment prospects of men facing poverty and social exclusion have worsened since the 1980s. Traditional industrial areas have been particularly badly affected by job losses, and large numbers of men of working age have become 'economically inactive' rather than registered unemployed. The problems facing young men and men from ethnic minorities in entering the labour market are particularly acute.

Education and training programmes are no panacea for the problems created by economic restructuring in recent years. Nevertheless, they have a place in helping men to adjust to changing circumstances, based on a realistic understanding of current labour market conditions and a commitment to the development of proper jobs.

Although men have generally been beneficiaries of investment in their human capital in recent years (see Chapter 4), this study found little emphasis on gender being consciously recognised as a key organising principle for the design, delivery, or evaluation of mainstream employment training to men on low incomes. The impact of stereotyped assumptions about appropriate roles was also evident. This gender-blindness is surprising, given the huge gender gap in participation in the different New Deal programmes, and the significant resources being invested by government in this area of work.

The internal barriers to effective take-up of education and training programmes by many men (especially older men) appear to consist of a lack of understanding of, or resistance to, retraining owing to fears of failure; dominant notions of the breadwinner role; ill-health and disability; and caring responsibilities. External barriers are also significant, including lack of access to transport; centralised training models taking insufficient account of gender; and local labour market conditions. Young men in particular often regard wages as too low, despite the introduction of the minimum wage. Training is also frequently seen as not 'macho', and schools and careers services pay little attention to addressing central issues of masculinity which underpin young men's attitudes.

Although some innovative approaches are being developed which have an intrinsic understanding of gender issues (even if no formal gender policies are in place), such projects are on a relatively small scale. The available evidence suggests that, alongside broader efforts to tackle outdated gender stereotypes, the development of targeted provision to address the needs of different groups of men should be promoted.

6
Men and health inequalities

In the 1998 consultation paper 'Our Healthier Nation', the government set out the case for 'concerted action to tackle not just the causes of disease, but the causes of the causes: poverty, inequalities, social exclusion, unemployment, and the other features of the physical and social environment that converge to undermine health'.[1]

The links between poverty, inequality, and health – and in particular men's health – are reinforced by the findings of research published in 2000 by Mitchell, Dorling, and Shaw.[2] The study suggested that if 'full employment' (based on the government's preferred definition that, while people may be temporarily between jobs, no-one is in long-term receipt of unemployment benefit) were achieved in Britain, some 2,500 deaths per year among those aged less than 65 would be prevented, and 83 per cent of the lives saved would be male. Moreover, a modest redistribution of wealth would prevent around 7,600 deaths each year (and would return inequalities in mortality to their 1983 levels). Again, men would benefit more than women, with 75 per cent of the lives saved being male.

Helping to explain these findings, The Men's Health Forum (MHF) (see box on page 52) highlights that men are at greater risk of premature death for biological reasons, lacking the protective effect oestrogen offers women against heart disease. MHF also argues that unemployment is a key factor affecting men's health, and that health services have, in general, not succeeded in providing the kinds of services that effectively target large numbers of men. MHF suggests that '... men take more risks with their health, such as drinking alcohol excessively and have having a poor diet, and are much less likely to report health problems to a health professional'.[3] Men also tend to have less access to supportive social networks than women, and this is especially likely for men who are unemployed (and therefore excluded from workplace networks).

While efforts to boost employment may improve men's health, this chapter suggests that the converse is true too: efforts to improve men's health may also have an impact by improving their employability, and addressing their poverty and social exclusion. The chapter begins by outlining some aspects of health inequality, and stresses in particular the negative health outcomes for men in the lowest social classes. It then explores key concerns around men's health in different age groups, and highlights examples of positive practice.

The context of men's health

Poverty is clearly disempowering. Yet men in our culture are supposed to be powerful and in control. The 'role strain' this dissonance is likely to create for many men can lead to both emotional stress and low self-esteem, with consequences for mental and physical health, and risk-taking behaviours, which are believed to compensate for feelings of emasculation. These behaviours can include drinking heavily, driving dangerously, unsafe sex, acts of violence, etc.

Peter Baker, Men's Health Forum, in an Oxfam GB seminar on Men and Poverty, Oxford, March 2001

Over the past decade or so, awareness has been growing steadily of men's health issues. Although there is evidence that some health differences between men and women are narrowing as women increasingly copy men's lifestyle choices (for example, by smoking and drinking more), the divergence in the overall trends remains significant. Some of the statistics highlighted most often are:

- men's greater mortality from heart disease;
- men's shorter life expectancy;
- men's higher rates of injury from accidents;
- men's and boys' higher suicide rates;
- and men's higher rates of alcohol abuse.

Further analysis of health outcomes for different groups of men reveal that they vary significantly according to age, ethnic background, class, and so on. It is younger men who are more likely to die as a result of accidents, for example, (including car accidents, fires, drowning, and poisoning). Higher rates of diabetes are reported in men from all the ethnic minority groups. Especially relevant to the current research is that men in social classes IV and V generally experience the worst health problems, as do men from some ethnic minority groups.

Inequality in life expectancy between social classes has widened over the last 20 years. Life expectancy at birth for all men in England and Wales rose by nearly five years between 1972-1976 and 1992-1996. The rise for men in social class I, the 'professional' class, was above this, at almost six years, while the rise for men in social class V, 'unskilled manual', was less than two years. By 1992-1996 the gap between the professional and unskilled manual classes was almost 10 years.

National Statistics, *Social Focus on Men*, The Stationery Office, 2001

It is also important to acknowledge that, although men as a group do fare worse on the measures above, in other ways they fare roughly the same as, or better, than women. For instance, official figures indicate that women have higher rates of severe disability than men, they are more prone to minor physical illness, and they have higher rates of mental illness (especially anxiety and depression).[4]

The 1998 Acheson Inquiry, set up by the government, concluded that: 'These differences between and within genders have important policy implications. They suggest that policies which decrease socio-economic inequalities will have a differential effect by decreasing male mortality, and particularly mortality in more disadvantaged men. They also suggest the need for gender specific policies to reduce inequalities, because the causes of inequalities may be different for men and women.'[5] The report went on to identify mortality in young men in particular as a key area where gender interacts with social inequalities, resulting in ill-health (alongside psychosocial ill-health in disadvantaged women with young children, and high levels of disability in older women).

Research by evolutionary psychologist Richard Wilkinson reinforces this emphasis on tackling inequality, suggesting that people in more egalitarian societies tend to be less hostile and violent to each other, and less subject to stress. For men in particular, he believes that the great difference between those with high and low status in hierarchical societies is a significant source of stress and therefore of ill-health. However his claims are contested and it has been argued that his focus on the psychological rather than the material effects of inequality is misplaced.[6]

Sixteen per cent of men were found to have a severe lack of social support (in the 1999 Health Survey for England), compared with 11 per cent of women. But there were social factors other than gender that had a greater effect on how much social support people received. While 13 per cent of men with 'high' household income (£13,365 or more a year) perceived that they had a severe lack of social support, 25 per cent of men in the 'lowest' household income group (less than £6,075) perceived that they had such a lack ... Among Chinese men, three-fifths in the low household income group perceived that they had a severe lack of social support. However, so too did almost a quarter of those in the highest income group. In nearly all of the Asian minority ethnic groups, higher proportions of men perceived that they had a severe lack of social support than those in the general population for all three household income levels.

National Statistics, *Social Focus on Men*, The Stationery Office, 2001

Neil Davidson of Working With Men confirmed these findings in an interview for this study, suggesting that men's health can be a significant entry point for tackling poverty and social exclusion. He also argued that only a few health projects have gender policies in place, and that a gender analysis is therefore not generally embedded within organisations. A survey he recently carried out of 21 agencies working with young men (most of them counselling organisations), found that almost two thirds of them felt that an awareness of masculinity played little or no part in their work with young men, or that they had not thought about the issue specifically.[7]

Although the government has taken some steps to reduce health inequalities (such as the introduction of national targets in relation to infant mortality and life expectancy), it has been reluctant to accept in full the wide-ranging recommendations of the Acheson Report (increases in benefit levels, for example). Nevertheless, it has made some initial moves towards addressing key aspects of men's health. For example, it is seeking to ensure that health promotion campaigns are aimed at boys and men as well as women and families (in relation to teenage pregnancy, and flu jabs, for instance), and this awareness should be extended. The Health Development Agency has been asked to look at what works in terms of improving men's health, and two interim reports comprising practice examples and key learning points were produced in 2001 by Working With Men on this overall theme. [8]

Although the focus on men's health has been limited so far, Health Action Zones have been set up in 26 disadvantaged areas to tackle health inequalities and to link health initiatives to regeneration, housing, employment, education, and anti-poverty initiatives. These could provide an important focus for further work on men's health in future. Already, for instance, there is evidence that in 1999-2000 in England, 5,429 men set a quit date through smoking cessation services in Health Action Zones, and of these, 41 per cent had successfully given up smoking at the four week follow-up stage.[9]

Despite these positive moves, a coherent gender perspective that embraces men is largely missing from government health strategies such as the NHS Plan,[10] Tackling Health Inequalities,[11] the National Strategy for Sexual Health and HIV,[12] and the National Service frameworks.[13]

The Men's Health Forum (MHF)

MHF was founded in 1994, and works to improve men's health by bringing together and working with the widest possible range of interested organisations and individuals. The Forum is now a well-established group with over 100 members drawn from a wide range of companies, charities, professional bodies, universities, and patient groups. It has produced several reports on key aspects of men's health, including 'Young Men and Suicide' (April 2000) and 'Inequalities in Health' (May 2000). The Forum aims to:

• improve the health of men by providing a platform for interested organisations and individuals to raise awareness, to discuss, disseminate, and promote ideas and information on men's health, and to develop good practice;

• develop research and educational strategies for identifying men's health initiatives;

• encourage men's health initiatives;

• facilitate discussion, networking, alliances, and the exchange of ideas on men's health policy, practice and issues;

• fully support equal opportunities (in respect of race, gender, sexuality, disability, age, etc.) in every aspect of its work;

• fully support improvements in women's and children's health. The Forum does not believe that men's healthcare can or should be improved by diverting resources from women's or children's healthcare services.

MHF has a website which provides information on a range of men's health projects, latest conferences, newsletters and reports, and a discussion area. Among the initiatives the Forum is developing is the first national Men's Health Week in the UK, based on the model developed in the USA.

In 2001, a linked Men's Health Forum Scotland (MHFS) was launched, reflecting the importance of men's health issues north of the border. For example, Glasgow suffers some of the worst poverty and corres-pondingly the highest morbidity and mortality rates in the UK. Formerly dependent on heavy industry, Glasgow's men have been particularly affected by socio-economic changes and the impact of these on traditional male roles. So far MHFS has received a grant for £180,000 from the Scottish Executive over three years, representing half of the funds necessary for the development of a Scotland-wide Men's Health Project (to be managed jointly by Community Health UK and MHFS), which will focus on the unemployed, those living in poverty, black and ethnic minorities, men in the workplace, and the young.

Young men's mental health

In recent research, Coleman and Schofield identify that girls and young women are twice as likely as boys to suffer a depressive disorder, ten times more likely to suffer from anorexia, and more likely to feel lonely. Young men are three times more likely to be dependent on alcohol, and twice as likely to be dependent on drugs.[14] Meltzer *et al.* suggest that among males, those aged 20-24 are thought to be at particular risk, and identify a strong association between mental health problems and unemployment.[15]

The evidence also suggests that young black men are over-represented in the mental health statistics (especially in relation to schizophrenia),[16] and that particular problems face Afro-Caribbean men (such as a greater likelihood of hospital admissions, contact with psychiatric services, and compulsory admittance to locked wards). It has been suggested that such discrepancies in the statistics are as a result of a range of factors including misdiagnosis, institutional racism, and the stereotyping of young black men as criminals.[17]

A central concern in relation to men's health is the number of men, especially young men, who commit suicide. Over the last 25 years, the suicide rate for men aged 15-24 has more than doubled.[18] Meanwhile, the number of suicides among women and older men has decreased significantly. According to a report from the Samaritans, the backgrounds of young men who self-harm are characterised not only by family problems, but also by social conditions: 'Within the wider social environment, when the prevalence of risk factors rise, such as unemployment, family breakdown, criminality, substance abuse, then these in turn will be associated with increasing rates of depression and suicidal behaviour.'[19]

A survey of health authorities conducted by the Men's Health Forum,[20] identified that only a few have strategies in place to attempt to reduce suicides, and that many find it difficult to design and implement appropriate policies. The Forum argues that a suicide strategy must address young men's specific interests, activities, and emotions. For example, services should be made more appropriate and attractive to young men, and staff should be encouraged to develop a positive approach and understanding of young men, rather than operate on the basis of negative stereotypes. Health services should also identify the images and messages that succeed in attracting young men's attention, and use these in suicide prevention work.

CALM: The Campaign Against Living Miserably

CALM embraces an innovative and positive approach to getting through to young men aged 15-35. By utilising current trends in youth culture, and by engaging with role models, CALM raises awareness of depression and suicide among young men, and encourages them to 'open up'. A free-phone helpline offers one source of support specific to young men, as well as signposting to other services, locally and nationally. An interactive website is also available at www.thecalmzone.net Launched by the Department of Health across Manchester in 1997, the campaign has expanded to Merseyside and Cumbria in 2000, and Bedfordshire in 2001, co-funded by local health commissioners.

The campaign's success lies in the way the message is marketed to young men, and the associations made with contemporary youth culture. Appealing to this audience involves creating an image and a brand that is credible and hard-hitting, moving away from traditional health messages and making what is on offer appear more appropriate to their own lifestyles.

Key elements of this approach include delivering relevant messages in the right language, and using traditional advertising and 'ambient' media: urinal posters ask their captive audience if they are 'Pissed Off?'; radio advertisements resonate with isolated listeners, repeating 'Is there anyone out there?' and 'please respond'; and beer mats pose the question 'Had enough?'. Visibility in the right places is essential: including in clubs and bars, football stadiums, record and clothes shops, and at gigs and festivals. A local presence is also vital as some young men may rarely leave the immediate area in which they live. Young men's negative perceptions of health services mean that role-models from the worlds of music and sport who endorse the message are one step ahead of health professionals in persuading young men to talk about problems. In this way, the campaign is associated with the things that young men aspire to, thus subtly reducing the stigma associated with talking about problems and asking for help.

Since the launch of CALM, the helpline counsellors have taken over 25,000 calls. Two-thirds of these are from men, reversing the usual pattern of calls to helplines. More than half of callers are not in touch with any other services, and though successful as a first port of call, it is essential that more specialist services are developed for young men – CALM is only as effective as the services it refers men to.

Pippa Sargent, National CALM Co-ordinator, taken from articles on the MHF website (www.menshealthforum.org.uk) and in *Working With Young Men* magazine, Volume 1, January 2002

These recommendations echo the findings of Davidson in his broader review of the response of mental health services to young men.[21] He argues that agencies fall into three main categories: a small number that are gender-blind; a second larger group that does recognise the need for further work with young men, but is not currently planning any; and a third much smaller group who are experimenting with broadening their overall approach and the range of services offered (such as detached workers, and groups for specific kinds of young men). Davidson concludes that a wide-ranging strategy is necessary to develop ways to help young men use services earlier and more effectively. This is especially the case in relation to mental illness, where the associated stigma makes men even less likely to ask for help from services.

42nd Street

The 42nd Street project provides a good example of an agency that has developed a coherent approach. Offering community-based support to young people aged 14-25 under stress in Manchester, Salford, and Trafford, the project has a strong focus on gender and sexuality. Four staff work specifically with young men at present, and men's groups have been run regularly. It also works extensively with Afro-Caribbean men and Muslim men, varying methods to meet the specific needs of each group. Approaches include individual counselling and informal support-group work in a range of settings such as youth clubs, and increasingly in schools. As with other projects working with young men, the workers confirmed the importance of talking with young men in their own language if they are to respond. They also highlighted the importance of an awareness of self-harm, and the centrality of this theme for many young men who want to take risks by hurting themselves and shutting off their feelings (whether through joy-riding, or becoming victims of violence in clubs, or putting themselves at risk of HIV).

Sexual health and young men

Boys often feel left out of family sex education. Fathers rarely talk to their sons on sexual and personal matters. Mothers may not know enough about boys' development. Many boys complain that sex education does not address their need to talk about sex in the context of relationships and emotions. Where services are designed specifically for young people and aimed at both sexes, only a small proportion of the clients are young men. Some boys present themselves as 'knowing it all' and mask their ignorance, vulnerabilities, and their need for help, advice, and support.

Home Office, 'Supporting Families: A consultation document', www.homeoffice.gov.uk/vcu/suppfam.htm, 1998

In 1999, the Social Exclusion Unit published a report on teenage pregnancy,[22] outlining the government's aims of reducing under-18 conceptions by half by 2010, and reducing the social exclusion of young parents by improving their support and access to education, training, and employment. One key focus is on targeting a publicity campaign at young men, encouraging them to take more responsibility for their sexual health and activity. Subsequent government guidance on sex and relationships education has also emphasised the importance of addressing boys' needs.

In Wales, which has the highest rates of teenage pregnancy in Britain, the Assembly has developed a 'Sexual Health Strategy for Wales'.[23] Some have criticised the inadequate attention within it to poverty and social exclusion, arguing that young men's marginalisation as a result of the loss of traditional roles in the family and community is leading to isolation and a loss of self-esteem. This has led to confusion regarding sexuality, sexual health, and relationships.[24] A parallel Sexual Health and HIV Strategy has followed in England, which identifies the particular needs of boys and young men, and acknowledges that service development and education in sexual health must take their needs into account.[25]

It is important that such messages should be implemented by well-designed interventions at grassroots level, building on formal sex education in schools. This is especially important, as failure to address boys' needs has serious implications for their emotional and sexual health; approaches that do not engage boys leave them bored and sometimes disruptive. It appears that a focus on the reproductive aspects of sex education engages girls but not boys; this can reinforce the message that sex education is nothing to do with boys.[26] Boys tend to respond to practical, informal, skills-based approaches.

> The Strategy fails to engage with sociological aspects of men's sexual health. Many men feel marginalised as a result of losing traditional roles within the family and community. This can lead to a loss of self-esteem, confidence, and an increase in isolation, which in turn may lead to drug and alcohol use and confusion with regards to sexuality, sexual health, and relationship issues.
>
> fpa Cymru, 'Report of the Consultation Day on the Sexual Health Strategy for Wales', February 2000

There is some evidence of the development of innovative approaches to target young men. For example, the Strides project is run by fpa Cymru (Family Planning Association Wales) in the south Wales valleys, where the highest levels of teenage pregnancy in Wales can be found. It works with socially excluded young men aged 13-20, running courses of 8-12 sessions of between one and two hours, to help them take responsibility for their sexual and emotional health, and to equip them with the skills

Traditionally the focus has been on girls. Boys may have felt embarrassed to ask questions about relationships or sex. Boys are also less likely to talk to their parents about sex and relationships.

Department for Education and Employment, 'Sex and Relationship Education Guidance', DfEE, 2000 and confidence to make informed choices. While issues like contraception, sexually transmitted infections, and testicular cancer provide the initial entry point, discussions inevitably also explore other key issues in their lives, such as attitudes to fatherhood, relationships, sexuality, homophobia, and being a man. This is seen by project staff as particularly worthwhile, given the importance of the industrial legacy of the 'macho' ideal, the strength of homophobia, and the embedded culture of low expectations and poor job opportunities for young men in the area. A particularly important feature of the project is the focus on finding appropriate ways of reaching young men and encouraging them to use services. According to the project staff, it is essential to go to places where young men go (usually via outreach work), to address the young people's agenda, to use male workers, and to use humour in talking to them.[27]

> *I'm a lot wiser now. Sessions give you a chance to talk about things you can't talk about anywhere else. The good thing is that my friends come to me for advice now because they know I've done the course. I feel more confident. It's opened my mind to a lot of different things and I'm enjoying it. I think all blokes should do this course!*

Young man on the Strides project, quoted in S. Siskos and S. Hughes, 'One Small Stride for Mankind ...', *Working With Men* journal No. 3, 2000

Improving the health of men in other age groups

Much attention rightly focuses on health issues facing young men, but there is also increasing recognition of the need to address the needs of other age groups. It appears that men (especially older men) living in deprived areas tend to consult their GP only when diseases such as cancer are more advanced, either due to lack of awareness or because they do not have the confidence to ask the doctor questions when the initial symptoms occur. Living in substandard housing, poor diet, and smoking and drinking, may also mean that immunity to fight disease is reduced.

The government is increasingly targeting prostate cancer (the second biggest killer of men in terms of cancers), boosting research funding, and piloting a prostate cancer risk-management programme for England, which will include the first standardised testing for prostate cancer in this country. And given that two-thirds of deaths from heart disease are of men, the government is also opening rapid access chest-pain clinics. But overall, the evidence suggests the need for wider measures to address poverty and social exclusion, if health inequalities are to be tackled.

> Heart disease is an illness that is strongly associated with deprivation. For men in all age groups between 35 and 74, the more deprived the area in which they lived, the more likely they were to develop coronary heart disease. In the 45 to 54 age group, 21 per 1,000 male patients from the least deprived areas were treated for heart disease, compared with 39 per 1,000 patients in the most deprived areas.
>
> National Statistics, *Social Focus on Men*, The Stationery Office, 2001

At local level, an increasing number of projects is also being initiated to address men's health needs more broadly. The Men's Health Forum Internet site currently gives details of 87 projects across the UK. For example:

- Tackling Health in Warrington seeks to disseminate information via amateur rugby league clubs in the area.
- Open for Men is a Well Man clinic in Lewisham: any man can attend on a Friday evening for a confidential discussion with a nurse, doctor, or counsellor.
- Alive and Kicking in the West Midlands registers individuals through Sunday football leagues, and encourages them to take part in various health-related tasks.
- Keeping it Up in Dorset ran a competition between local workplaces, with teams made up of overweight men aged 40-55, each earning points for reducing their percentage body fat.
- Pilot Project in Pubs held clinics in pubs, betting shops, and other public places in the West Midlands, screening men for excessive smoking, drinking, obesity, and high blood pressure.

Working With Men/Paul Leatham

Men's Health Highland

Men s Health Highland is a charity which aims to promote awareness of men's health issues. With a population of 50,000 living mostly in rural communities, the Highland region covers a relatively large area of Scotland. Many men face difficulties in accessing mainstream health provision such as Well Man clinics, and the project works to raise awareness through a range of means (for example, leaflet drops, and lunchtime workplace sessions). Themes include heart disease, smoking, and prostate cancer.

Although raising awareness of such issues is not a new notion, it appears that the message has in some way been failing to be picked up by those at which it is aimed. This may be indicative of the way in which many men view healthcare and health issues. Stereotypical notions of what men are supposed to do, and what it means to be manly and masculine remain pervasive. In the Highlands, where farming is a wide-spread industry, traditional notions of masculinity may be more deeply entrenched than in other areas. Thus drinking is widespread among many men in the area, an issue about which the project continues to promote awareness. Suicides among men are also greater here than in any other region of Scotland.

A major role of the project is to raise awareness of preventative medicine. The experience of the support worker is that men are more reluctant than women to address such issues and are less likely to ask for help, even if it is required. As a result, the Men's Health Highland project seeks to raise awareness with women about the need for their male partners to take an active interest in their own health. While this in some way reinforces the notion that women are responsible for the health and well-being of the family (the stereotypical caring role), the ultimate aim is to encourage men to be responsible for their own well-being.

In attempting to make healthcare and health information as available and accessible to men as it is for women, the project indirectly promotes a policy informed by gender equality. By encouraging men to be aware and responsible for their own healthcare, the project in turn advocates a changing status for women by dismantling traditional, stereotypical notions of women and femininity.

J. Mawson, unpublished report for Oxfam GB on work with men in Scotland, 2000

Overall, therefore, a range of initiatives is being implemented across the UK to address men's health. While the numbers of such projects are growing, significant challenges remain both to bring such initiatives into the mainstream, and to encourage men to take greater interest in their health. Though significantly more information about men's health is becoming available, particularly on the Internet, it is a struggle to get men to engage with this area. This is especially the case for men in low-income groups, who do not generally have Internet access. This brief review suggests that it is essential to seek to target these men in the places they regularly visit (as does the Pilot Project in Pubs described above) and to base health-promotion activities on men's particular need and experiences.

Developing health policy

Beyond specific intervention through health agencies, it is also vital to remember that tackling health inequalities is not only a matter for health policy, but also for wider social policy to address. The Minister for Public Health, Yvette Cooper MP, reinforced this recently in relation to men on low incomes:

> The health of men on high incomes is improving. They're closing the gap with women. The area with most problems is that of men on low incomes. So it clearly is possible to improve men's health or to make a difference, because for some men, that's what is happening. The New Deal for the over 50s or the young unemployed and other issues around tackling unemployment can have a huge impact on people's health and are as important, if not more important, than anything you can do directly through the health service.[28]

Building on this point, this study suggests that it also important to make more extensive links between different sectoral approaches. Given that men are the majority of attendees on the New Deal for Young People and the New Deal for the Long-term Unemployed, and that poor health is a major factor inhibiting men taking up work opportunities, it seems logical to suggest that a health component should be added to such programmes.

Such action needs to be complemented by more direct men's health-policy initiatives. For example, at the local level, health authorities are now obliged to produce Health Improvement Programmes identifying local strategies to tackle health inequalities. With one notable exception

(Worcestershire Health Authority), men's needs are not specifically addressed. Similarly, few of the 26 Health Action Zones partnerships (set up in 1998 and which operate in deprived areas) are targeting work with men, although Let's Get Serious is an exception (see Chapter 5).

Primary care also needs to be made more attractive to men, who tend to seek help and advice from medical practitioners later than women in the course of any given condition. It seems that many men prefer easily accessible clinics, preferably offering greater anonymity than the average GP surgery. Drop-in centres are one possibility and it will be interesting to see whether the recently established national network of NHS drop-in centres succeeds in attracting more men.[29] Similarly, it may be that the establishment of the telephone helpline NHS Direct may prove another effective means of engaging with men.

> ... There are also differences in GP consultation rates between minority ethnic groups. In 1999, 22 per cent of Bangladeshi men, 17 per cent of Indian men and 16 per cent of black Caribbean men had consulted a GP in the two weeks prior to interview in the Health Survey for England. Men in the Chinese and Irish minority ethnic groups had consultation rates similar to the figure for all men of 12 per cent.
>
> National Statistics, *Social Focus on Men*, The Stationery Office, 2001

Summary

Awareness of particular aspects of men's health such as the prevalence of heart disease, testicular cancer, alcohol abuse, suicides, and high overall mortality, has grown during the 1990s. These problems do not affect all men equally, however. For example, men in social classes IV and V and men in some ethnic minority groups experience the worst health problems. Although such figures are sometimes presented as proof of men's disadvantage in comparison with women, in fact women fare worse on other measures (they have higher rates of severe disability, mental illness, and minor physical illness, for example).

There is evidence to suggest that tackling inequality and poverty by achieving full employment and a modest redistribution of wealth in Britain would be of particular benefit in reducing male mortality. Attempts to address men's greater propensity to risk-taking behaviour (such as excessive drinking, poor diet, and obesity), and their unwillingness compared with women to use professional health services, are also worthwhile.

The evidence of this study confirms that men's health can be a significant entry point for tackling poverty and social exclusion. The government has taken some initial steps to address men's health, however a gender perspective is largely missing from government strategies such as the NHS Plan, Tackling Health Inequalities, the Sexual Health Strategy and the National Health Service frameworks, and the absence of gender-related health targets does little to encourage health providers to do more on men's health. Few projects or services have gender policies in place, and most therefore fail to respond to men's needs and concerns appropriately, or to find ways of engaging with men by addressing their agendas, going to places where they gather, using male workers, and skills-based training. Nevertheless, isolated examples of positive practice exist, and these should be replicated more widely.

7

The roots of men's violence

Given the structures of inequality that exist between men and women in contemporary developed countries (and elsewhere), Connell argues that it is hard to imagine such an unjust distribution of resources not being accompanied by violence. This violence emerges in two main patterns. On the one hand, many men, as members of the dominant group, use violence to sustain their position *vis-à-vis* women. On the other, violence can become a way of asserting masculinity in group struggles with other men. 'The youth gang violence of inner-city streets is a striking example of the assertion of marginalised masculinities against other men, continuous with the assertion of masculinity in sexual violence against women.'[1] Connell goes on to suggest that this latter 'protest masculinity' is shaped by class deprivation and lack of access to cultural or economic resources, and is rooted at heart in poverty.

Care is necessary here to distinguish the impact of poverty on the violence men display in particular situations. While gang culture and male-on-male violence is usually visible within a context of social deprivation, there is also evidence that certain other forms of violence, in particular violence against women, are often perpetrated by educated and successful men. Projects working in this field are understandably very wary of making any links between poverty and violence against women, as they feel that making this association can provide an excuse which violent men will use to deny responsibility for their actions. Having said this, Kimmel suggests that 'one of the best predictors of the onset of domestic violence is unemployment'.[2] If this is right, there are grounds for attempting to explore further the impact of men's socio-economic circumstances on their gender-based violence.

In this chapter, the statistical evidence linking men, offending, and violence is surveyed. Attempts by projects to challenge men's violence are then highlighted, especially in the field of domestic violence. Broader links between offending and masculinity are then explored, though there is less practical work here to draw upon in coming to any robust conclusions. Finally, the question of men as victims of violence is briefly addressed.

Gender and crime: the evidence

Undoubtedly, men commit more crimes of all types than women, and overall, more serious and violent crimes. This gulf has been consistent over time, and is repeated in the statistics of other countries. Consideration of the 'gendered' nature of crime has tended to focus on sexual violence and domestic violence, and the weight of evidence suggests that, overwhelmingly, the perpetrators of these types of crime are men and the victims are women (and children). Moreover, these crimes are extremely common. Based on evidence from the British Crime Survey and findings of a UK-wide snapshot survey, it has been suggested recently that 'an incident of domestic violence occurs in the UK every six to twenty seconds'.[3]

Appalling though this is, it is also essential to acknowledge that official UK data show that men's violence to men is by far the most prevalent form of violence. This encompasses, among other things, behaviour such as football hooliganism, alcohol-related violence, rioting, and racist and homophobic attacks.[4] Much of this violence (though by no means all) is perpetrated by young men living in low-income households, especially in areas of high unemployment and deprivation.

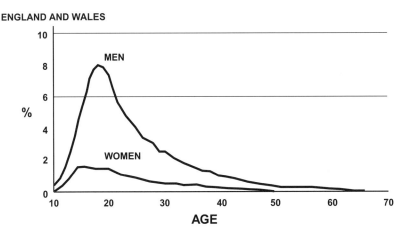

ENGLAND AND WALES

Figure 4:

Offenders* as a percentage of the population, by gender and age, 1999

*People found guilty or cautioned for indictable offences in 1999

Source: Home Office

> When we speak statistically of 'men' having higher rates of violence than women, we must not slide to the inference that therefore *all* men are violent. Almost all soldiers are men, but most men are not soldiers. Though most killers are men, most men never kill or even commit assault. Though an appalling number of men do rape, most men do not.
>
> R. Connell, *The Men and the Boys*, Polity, 2000

Despite the frequency with which such crimes are committed, careful examination of the evidence suggests that men's propensity to violence is not biologically derived. In fact the available research strongly supports the correlation between experiencing violence as a child and the propensity to use violence later in life.[5] Cross-cultural studies of masculinities reveal very diverse patterns, which are impossible to reconcile with simplistic biological determinism.[6]

It is also important to remember that although the fear of men's violence is endemic (especially among women) and has damaging social effects, in practice not all men are violent. This fact should be of great significance in constructing strategies for reducing men's violence, both in relation to work on general violence prevention (for example, media campaigns, legal reform, education and support for children and families, and anti-poverty measures), and to specific project intervention with those who use violence.

Challenging men's violence

In the areas of sexual and domestic violence (and to a lesser extent car crime among young men) the clear links between gender and crime, and the centrality of masculinities have begun to be addressed. This is evident in the emergence of the RESPECT Practitioners Network, which brings together a range of projects around the principle that 'the primary aim in working with perpetrators of domestic violence is to increase the safety of women and children'. This principle has been endorsed as good practice by the government's Women's Unit.[7] Building on this statement, RESPECT has developed a more detailed set of core values and principles.

RESPECT: 'Principles and Philosophy for Working With Men's Violence to Partners and Ex-partners'

- Domestic violence is unacceptable and must be challenged at all times.
- Men's violence to partners and ex-partners is largely about the misuse of power and control in the context of male dominance.
- Violence within same sex relationships or from women to men is neither the same as – nor symmetrically opposite to – men's violence to women.
- Men are responsible for their use of violence.
- Men can change.
- We are part of a community response, which needs to be consistent and integrated at all levels.
- Everyone affected by domestic violence should have access to support services.
- All work with perpetrators and victims of domestic violence must actively promote an alternative, positive and constructive model of human relationships.
- Practitioners working in the field of domestic violence should attempt to apply these principles to their own practice.

For further details, see www.changeweb.org.uk

A recent survey of RESPECT members and Probation Services provided mixed evidence on the approaches of nineteen perpetrator programmes across the UK.[8] It showed that:

- The majority of programmes had policies and procedures on domestic violence in place, although this was not the case for five projects.
- Nine projects took all referrals, and ten operated selection criteria to seek a degree of motivation.
- All the projects limited men's rights to confidentiality, so that partners could be given information about progress or risks to children's safety.
- Contact with women was routine, with all 19 programmes having direct links with support services for women, 15 running their own

linked partner-support, and all providing information about linked services for women and children. Seven projects had no child-protection policies, however.

- All groups claimed to avoid competing directly for funds with women's domestic violence services, though only eight had a written policy to this effect.

- Few programmes had clear or rigorous policies on referring non-attenders to court for breaching the terms of their orders.

- All 19 programmes had a domestic violence forum in their area, and all sent a designated liaison person to attend it.

Perhaps the best-known programme is that established by the CHANGE project, based in Stirling, which provided the original foundation for the RESPECT Network.

CHANGE (Men Learning to End Their Violence To Women) Ltd

Established in 1989, CHANGE aims to challenge and change the attitudes and actions of men who are violent to women. The first of its kind in Europe, the company has developed a men's programme, which works within the criminal justice system as an alternative to custodial or monetary punishment for such crimes. CHANGE implements these aims through the training of other agencies working with the perpetrators of domestic violence.

The central principle of the CHANGE scheme is that men's violence towards their female partners is '… intentional, albeit not always conscious, behaviour that men use to maintain power over and to control women in intimate relationships'.[9] The project comes from a highly gendered perspective; indeed CHANGE has been established to empower women directly. There is a deep understanding of issues affecting women victims and the work is focused to this end. By placing the rehabilitation scheme within the criminal justice system, a clear message is being given to women that there are institutional mechanisms in place to support and empower them. To men, the message is simply that such behaviour is unacceptable and criminal. This is a concerted effort to challenge the traditional, patriarchal assumptions held by some that male-on-female violence in the home is an acceptable and 'normal' element of family life.

Based on J. Mawson, unpublished study for Oxfam GB on Work with Men in Scotland, 2000

An in-depth evaluation of CHANGE and the Lothian Domestic Violence Probation Project explored the impact of the programme on male attendees, the majority of whom were long-term unemployed, in both cases. It found that, in contrast to other criminal justice sanctions, programmes for men who use violence can have significant effects on the prevalence and frequency of violence over a twelve-month period following the imposition of a sanction. This finding is in line with a number of evaluations of similar projects in the US. The researchers conclude that 'men's programmes are not a panacea, rather they can play a positive role in the overall complement of improved legal, social, medical and community responses'.[10]

Despite the existence of a national statement of good practice (which is itself unusual) and some examples of good practice, work with the perpetrators of domestic violence remains a controversial area. Research by Humphreys *et al.* has suggested that:

> There are fears that, if inappropriately conducted, it may divert abusers from facing full legal consequences; offer false hope to partners; teach perpetrators more subtle ways to intimidate; compete for funding with services for women and children; and be unaccountable to survivors. Overall its effectiveness is far from proven.[11]

From a different perspective, questions have been raised about the strong focus on standardised short-term structured educational programmes based almost entirely upon the dominant US 'Duluth' model.[12] There is little evidence to support such wide-scale adoption, especially within the UK legal and cultural context. Focusing on cognitive behaviour (that is, attempting to change men's reasoning) may be the most effective way to stop violence in the short term, but some have argued that long-term change requires a more holistic understanding which addresses the complex motivations of individual abusers.[13]

Based on his experience of working with over 150 violent men on the CHANGE programme, former joint co-ordinator Dave Morran suggests that although the premise is valid that men use abusive or violent behaviour to establish, maintain, or regain power, in reality many men struggle to recognise this picture of their lives as powerful. In fact, many men are not only frightening, but also afraid of themselves, largely because they do not know who they are, they are isolated from other men, and have never learned to speak meaningfully to other men.

Men are constantly fearful and anxious about themselves, and, fearful, will employ the tactics of abuse and violence to regain their power, ignoring the costs to themselves, their partners, their children, their relationships, their physical and mental health, their freedom.

Dave Morran, Stirling University, Oxfam GB seminar on Men and Poverty, Oxford, March 2001

They are also fearful that they cannot survive without women, on whom they depend for everything. Their relationships then become focused on control of women at all costs. Alongside behavioural work, it is therefore vital to address the complex feelings that underpin men's violence (which are linked to Connell's 'dominant models of masculinity'), not only through intervention programmes, but also within wider society.[14]

Ahimsa

One of a small but growing number of UK projects set up to address men's violence against known women is Ahimsa (formerly the EVERYMAN Centre), established in 1989. In 1996, the charity moved from its Brixton and north London premises to Plymouth, where it continues to offer a focused psycho-social counselling programme, informed by feminist perspectives and drawing on a wide range of theoretical and clinical disciplines. The majority of clients attend a 13-month-long core programme on a voluntary basis (free to Plymouth men over the age of 18), having referred themselves or been recommended by other voluntary or statutory agencies. The Centre also works in partnership with the Devon Probation Service, and a number of men participate in the programme as a condition of their probation orders.

The Centre provides a linked Women's Service for partners of men referred to the programme. The services share the same building (although women are interviewed elsewhere, if their preference or needs for safety dictate) in order to take advantage of economies of scale, to minimise splitting, and to maximise liaison.

A pilot study conducted by the Centre for Social Policy, based in Dartington, Devon, is just being completed. The researchers have interviewed a variety of ex-clients and (where safe to do so) their partners or ex-partners in an attempt to determine the difference the intervention has made. They conclude that the project is capable of making a dramatic impact on men and their relationships, even if they have dropped out before completion.

Based on information from the project's website, www.ahimsa.org.uk

Masculinity and offending: addressing the wider links

All our evidence suggests that for men, it is the violence found in pubs and clubs and from disputes and conflicts with friends and neighbours that harms men the most.

Professor Betsy Stanko, director ESRC Violence Research Programme, in *The Guardian*, 27 October 2000

Despite innovations such as those described above in relation to challenging men's violence to women, this study found little evidence of attempts within the key criminal justice agencies to address the links between masculinity and offending on a more systematic basis (although some innovative work has been done within the probation service over the past decade or so). Indeed, it has been argued that too great a concentration on tackling men's role in domestic violence alone may be limiting. As Potts has suggested:

> There will be a danger that, in attempting to take domestic violence more seriously, even if masculinity is addressed, then it may still be overlooked as a major factor in wider offending and, consequently, the understanding of most crime will continue to neglect gender.[15]

Campbell provides one explanation for this in highlighting how male staff within criminal justice agencies share common cultural characteristics with male offenders, and in effect collude in making masculinities invisible within the work that they do.[16]

This reality was illustrated by an interview conducted for this study with staff from the Social Work Unit at Barlinnie Prison in Glasgow. This showed that, even though the prisoners are all men, the prison is fundamentally gender-blind in its approach. Prison staff are often unaware of the specific crime that a prisoner has committed. Indeed, many men who have committed acts of violence against their female partner will be imprisoned for a non-specific crime (for example, 'breach of the peace'), or their prison record card may simply state 'violent assault'. Given that resources for therapeutic interventions are lacking for all but a few, men who use violence are therefore not assisted to take any responsibility for their actions. In many cases the prison acts merely as a holding pen in which the prisoners bide their time until release, then simply re-offend.

Beyond the sphere of domestic violence, there appear to be few practice examples to draw upon where masculinity is addressed as a specific topic within programmes to tackle offending. A wide-ranging survey by the Probation Inspectorate of probation programmes working with white working class men argued that 'increasing attention is being paid to the links between masculinity and offending'. Nevertheless it went on to indicate that 'there is not yet an evidence base that would require those issues to be covered in all general offending programmes for men'.[17]

Although experience is limited, positive project work has been undertaken. In the 1990s, for example, a Men and Offending Group was run at Camberwell Probation Centre in inner London alongside a cognitive training programme. Evaluations showed that it was a very effective way of engaging male offenders and helping them to develop self-awareness and reflection.[18] Similar work has been taken forward more recently at Sherbourne House Probation Centre.

Sherbourne House Probation Centre

Sherbourne House works with young men aged between 16 and 20, whose offending behaviour has placed them at risk of custody. Offenders come from the whole of the Inner London area, and attend the programme as a direct alternative to custody based on a court requirement.

The main aim of the programme is to reduce offending by:

- encouraging young offenders to take responsibility for their actions;
- increasing self-confidence and self-esteem;
- and enabling young offenders to make realistic and positive choices about their future.

Offenders attend the centre four-and-a-half days a week for a period of ten weeks. The programme consists of 70 per cent group work, and 30 per cent education, training, and employment. The main elements of the programme are:

- offending behaviour groups;
- masculinity and offending groups;
- skills for living;

- education, training, and employment;
- and multi-racial, black self-development, and race discrimination groups.

The 'masculinity and offending' sessions provide a unique opportunity for the young men to examine how traditional ideas of masculinity have shaped their environment, and in doing so, limited their behaviour, outlook, and attitudes according to the expectations laid down by society. The aim of the sessions is to create a safe environment in which they can reflect on 'being a man' with other young men. Hopefully, by the end of the programme, they are able to start making links between the process of male socialisation and offending. An obvious example is the way in which groups will often equate the role of the provider with 'being a man'. If employment is difficult to obtain, offending is an option that can help men meet this expectation, and gain status and the other rewards that serve to reinforce their male identity.

Based on article at
www.hda-online.org.uk/yphnnews/issue10/content/focus_a.html

Outside the formal criminal justice agencies, innovative approaches have also been developed (for example, by youth services). In Northern Ireland, for instance, YouthAction received funding in 2000 from the Peace and Reconciliation Programme's initiative on 'Young Men and Violence'. This was used to carry out consultations with young men aged 14 to 25 to research their thoughts and perspectives on violence. Six pilot programmes were then set up in partnership with local groups to explore how young men could identify potential alternatives to violence, and the findings were then published and shared with practitioners and other agencies; the young men themselves playing a key role in the process.[19]

The work raised important issues for practice. The majority of the young men argued that they had never discussed or reflected on violence or the impact it has on them and their lives. It was therefore crucial to create supportive environments where they could do this, with skilled workers who would approach young men positively.

While these recommendations do have general application, it is important to acknowledge that there are some risks here. In practice, the responses of practitioners can sometimes reinforce 'macho' values if they are not careful. For example, it has been suggested that working with young male offenders can sustain a male worker's own image as 'strong' and 'tough'; as a result, he can avoid challenging, or may easily reinforce, the behaviour of the young men he works with. At the same time, he may marginalise the needs of women workers and offenders.[20]

Red Ladder Theatre Company

In 1998, Red Ladder was supported by Oxfam to write and tour with a play called 'Wise Guys', a hard-hitting urban drama targeting young men. It explored the conflicting emotions of contemporary youth in working class communities in Britain. The play was developed with young men and looked at male identity, focusing particularly on the reasons for and the results of criminal and violent behaviour. Rather than taking a moral standpoint, the play explored the idea that young men and boys do have choices, and can take opportunities to look at what they are doing, and make it different.

The play toured the north and midlands of England, and Scotland, and reached around 4,000 young people. The company employs actors who are at ease mixing with young people and engage with them before and after the performance. The production package included preparation and materials for follow-up, drawing on *The Oxfam Gender Training Manual.*[21] The play is a starting point for audience discussion of the profound changes in gender roles that are affecting their communities.

See also information in *Links* (Oxfam GB's newsletter on gender), July 1998 www.oxfam.org.uk/policy/gender/98jul/987male.htm

Men as victims

Men are also more likely than women to be victims of crime. Young men aged 16 to 24 are most likely to be the victims of violent crime, possibly as a result of being in places where violence can occur, such as pubs, or in groups late at night. According to the latest British Crime Survey estimates, in 1999, men of all ages in England and Wales were three times more likely than women to suffer 'stranger violence', that is, at the hands of an unknown assailant. Most victims of domestic violence are women, although it is recognised that this does happen to men, as does stalking.

National Statistics, *Social Focus on Men*, The Stationery Office, 2001

While official statistics suggest that men are very often the targets of physical violence, it is only in recent years that the impact of such violence on men's lives has begun to be understood. In contrast, a wealth of material is already available illustrating the impact on women of men's violence.

In addition to gender as a factor in victimisation, there appears to be a link with low income. Households located on council estates and having a low income are generally the most likely to be victims of burglary and violent crime, while those living in affluent and suburban areas are the least likely.[22]

Research on men's experiences by Stanko and Hobdell suggests that male victims of assault view their victimisation through a male frame, the essence of which sees victimisation as 'weak and helpless'.[23] They argue that this creates difficulties for men in expressing feelings, leaving them isolated and unable to ask for support. Furthermore, in comparison with women who tend to internalise blame, men tend to externalise it; this may result in feelings of anger, which can be a problem for others.

This study found evidence that some services, often those which originally worked with women, are increasingly attempting to meet the needs of male victims too. For example, New Pathways in Merthyr Tydfil in south Wales is a small counselling agency working with victims of violence and sexual abuse, which began in 1993 as a telephone helpline and women's organisation. The project started taking men a year ago, and about 20 of its 170 clients are men. According to project staff, the loss of jobs in the valleys has led to the abuse of power in other spheres, such as family violence. In addition, levels of homophobia are high in the area, and male rape victims are often unwilling to report offences against them.

Similarly, the Dunfermline Area Abuse Survivors Project (DAASP) was originally set up to offer support and counselling to female survivors of childhood sexual abuse throughout Fife, but its service has now been extended to male survivors too. Initially it was older men who were utilising the project, however the age range is now across the spectrum with the youngest male survivor being currently seventeen years old. At present it is estimated that men account for around 50 per cent of survivors using the service. Most approach the project directly, but some are referred by other agencies. Much of the work is one-to-one counselling, support, or befriending. However the project also organises mixed-sex user forums, which have apparently proved to be a useful addition, allowing both men and women to explore stereotypical views of gender.

Such initiatives tend to be small-scale, but they do seem to be filling a gap in service-provision. Nevertheless, they appear to be under-funded, and struggling to survive in a very competitive environment. Although such projects are increasingly working with both men and women, this study did not get a sense that they have a developed gender analysis. Rather, they tend not to differentiate between the sexes, seeing both men and women as potential victims. It is suggested that these projects would benefit from developing clearer gender policies and practice statements, building on the example provided by domestic violence-perpetrator projects.

Summary

Men commit far more crimes, and more violent crimes, than women. Most of these crimes are committed by disadvantaged young men against other young men (e.g. football hooliganism, alcohol-related violence, racist and homophobic attacks), often in areas of high unemployment and deprivation. Sexual and domestic violence, however, is usually committed by men against women and children, and perpetrators tend to come from all classes.

The importance of masculinity as a key factor underpinning men's offending has been most often explored in relation to gender-based violence, prompted by demands made by local women's groups for increased protection. For example, the RESPECT Network brings together a range of projects across the UK around a set of core principles, prioritising the safety of women and children. These programmes therefore tend to be rooted in a developed gender analysis. Nevertheless, they remain controversial, as their effectiveness is far from proven (although some evaluations, for example, of the CHANGE project in Stirling, have shown positive outcomes), and it is as yet unclear which models are the most successful.

There is also some evidence that masculinity is often overlooked by mainstream services as a key factor in men's violent offending. Although some innovative work is taking place in the probation service, overall approaches tend to remain relatively gender-blind. Indeed, the male-dominated institutions of the criminal justice system can often reinforce rather than challenge 'macho' attitudes and practices among male offenders.

Beyond these intervention strategies, it is essential too to develop more wide-ranging approaches to violence prevention. These should focus on areas such as media campaigns, legal reform, education and support for children and families, and anti-poverty measures.

8
Increasing the focus on fathers

Over the past decade or more, fatherhood has been at the forefront of policy debate surrounding the family. In the early 1990s, the emphasis of the 1989 Children Act on the importance of parental responsibility, active parenting, and the principle of the best interests of the child tended to be overshadowed by increasing political and public concern with 'feckless fathers' or father absence, rising at times to widespread 'moral panic'. Fuelling this trend was the work of 'underclass' theorists such as Murray in the USA,[1] and Dennis and Erdos in the UK,[2] who argued controversially that there is a link between the rise in the numbers of fatherless families and rising crime rates, with men's behaviour becoming increasingly uncivilised and irresponsible, largely as a result of growing female independence and the decline of marriage. This was one of the factors which led to the introduction of the 1991 Child Support Act, which sought to bolster the traditional provider role of biological fathers, based on the view that they must pay maintenance to support their children, and reduce the cost to the State of supporting growing numbers of lone parent mothers.

From the mid-1990s, a separate discourse began to emerge, which explored men's lack of involvement and practical commitment to parenting, high-lighting in particular personal and structural barriers to involved fatherhood.[3] In contrast to the pessimistic view of men inherent in the approach of Conservative administrations, this later approach, promoted by the left-leaning think-tank the Institute for Public Policy Research (IPPR), suggested a much more optimistic reading (some would say too optimistic[4]) of men's actual and potential contribution as fathers. This was based on principles such as the need to widen cultural images of fatherhood, improve education and support for fathers, adopt a children's rights perspective, and develop a legal framework to encourage men to be involved with their children. Under the subsequent Labour governments, the IPPR approach has tended to predominate; more supportive policy responses to fathers have been put in place, best symbolised by the introduction of a limited period of paid paternity leave.

Both of these approaches appear to underplay the impact of structural economic changes on fatherhood, and men's and women's responses to them. Whereas Murray, for instance, blames mothers (in particular single mothers) for undermining the civilising force of marriage on men, Campbell suggests that it is the response of working class men to unemployment and poverty that is the root cause of many social problems relating to fatherhood.[5] It has also been argued that the risks that a small number of fathers pose to women and children within families are being downplayed by an emphasis on containing the activities of predatory paedophiles within communities.[6]

This chapter highlights recent research and initiatives in relation to fatherhood; outlines the challenges facing welfare services in working with fathers; and sets out examples of practical initiatives to engage with them. It concludes that it is important to develop models of support appropriate to the needs of low-income fathers.

The context of fatherhood

Caring is a cause of financial poverty for women: lack of caring might be considered a cause of emotional poverty for men. The question remains whether we can envisage and move towards a society where caring is recognised and valued, and in which caring – both paid and unpaid – is compatible with good employment and a decent income.

Peter Moss, Thomas Coram Research Unit, Oxfam GB seminar on Men and Poverty, Oxford, March 2001

Against a background of an increase in the levels of employment among mothers, a steep rise in divorce rates, declining marriage rates, and more babies born outside marriage, a research review by Lewis provides the most comprehensive picture of the contribution fathers make to contemporary life.[7] He argues that such trends have upset stereotypical notions of men as breadwinning, disciplinarian fathers, and of mothers as non-earning housekeepers and carers, although these cultural images still exert a powerful influence in practice.

Yet despite the image of the 'absentee father' and historically high levels of divorce, seven out of ten families consist of dependent children living with both their birth parents. In terms of responsibility for childcare, middle class parents tend to express more egalitarian attitudes than working class parents. What happens in reality may be different, however: among those whose lives have been followed by the National Child Development Study since 1958, only 35 per cent of fathers with graduate qualifications said they took an equal share of childcare, compared with 58 per cent of men with few or no qualifications.

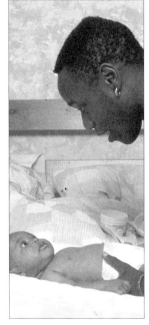

The reality of the organisation of household roles and responsibilities is a complex one, but strong evidence exists that early father involvement with a child is associated with continuing involvement with that child throughout childhood and adolescence. Father involvement is also associated with good parent-child relations, and is strongly related to positive later educational attainment. Children with involved fathers are less likely too to be in trouble with the police or to experience homelessness as an adult.[8]

For many fathers, however, their paid employment patterns are a significant factor in the extent to which they care for their children. In the UK they work the longest hours in the European Union (an average of 48 hours a week for those with children under 11),[9] and in spring 2000, a third of men with dependent children worked 50 or more hours a week.[10] It is also important to note that, despite increasing public focus on the importance of work-life balance, employment has become more intensified and stressful for both men and women over the past decade, limiting their capacity to be involved parents. Increases in the range of tasks and the quantity of work have been accompanied by a rise in unsocial hours and increasing fears of losing a job, especially in areas where traditional manufacturing industry has declined. Demands have multiplied for employees to travel and be accessible round the clock (whether in person, by email, video links, or telephone).[11] As Taylor has argued:

> ... a wide range of empirical evidence now exists that reveals there has
> been an unmistakable trend in Britain over the last ten years towards
> an intensification in the length and intensity of paid employment.
> Jobs in general are becoming more stressful.[12]

Despite these trends, 'successful' employment still appears to assume employees have no care responsibilities, or that care responsibilities should not interfere with work, and the full-time, continuous (male) worker remains the norm. The corollary is that women assume responsibility for caring even if employed, and part-time work or flexible working arrangements are less often taken up by men. In reality, fathers are often only confronted by significant caring responsibilities at times of transition, for example when they become non-resident or lone parents.

> ... the traditional male role as breadwinner has been seriously eroded and men find themselves in a changing culture where their wives are often the chief wage-earners, albeit in low-paid jobs, and the men remain at home with the responsibility of caring for the children.
>
> With the cultural expectations of fathers as providers and mothers as carers still entrenched despite the changing employment culture, many men are unprepared for the new role of fathers as parent and primary carer. They come to the role reluctantly and lacking in confidence, being thrown into the job for negative reasons. Their loss of self-esteem through ongoing unemployment, and sensitivity at their seeming inability to fulfil responsibilities as provider makes for unstable foundations from which to nurture their offspring.
>
> Fathers Plus, 'Involving Fathers', Children North-East, Newcastle, 2000

The picture varies for men in particular groups (such as unemployed fathers, young fathers, cohabiting fathers, non-resident fathers, stepfathers, and lone fathers), especially those who are socially excluded. While low pay or low income confront women in particular, when men are faced with these circumstances, it undermines their belief in whether they are able to be good providers, and for many, affects whether they see themselves as good fathers.[13]

This is especially the case for fathers who are outside the labour market. It appears, for example, that unemployed fathers, although they spend more time with their children, rarely take on a major role in housework and childcare after losing their jobs. Their lack of central involvement may be directly related to the reason they became unemployed, however, (for example, ill-health, or a family member's incapacity).

In contrast, non-resident fathers (of whom there are over 2 million in the UK), although often stereotyped as 'feckless', in many cases struggle hard to be involved fathers, despite being generally poorer than other fathers. According to research by Bradshaw *et al.*, they are also more likely to be unemployed, to have lower incomes even if employed, to be on benefits, to be younger, to have poorer health than fathers in general, and to have experienced multiple housing moves.[14] Yet in this research, contact with children was higher than expected, and almost half saw their children every week. In general, contact was more regular if the father was working, if the child was young, if the father had no new children and was living nearby, and if a good relationship was maintained with the mother. Similarly, many lone fathers (ten per cent of lone parents in the UK) are playing a much more active role in their children's upbringing than they did before becoming lone parents.[15]

Towards a new policy agenda

Changes such as those described above have helped to maintain father-hood on the policy agenda. Among the key themes, Lewis identifies that:

- legal definitions of fathering and fatherhood stress the importance of biological links between men and children;
- the debate about non-resident fathers has focused on men's economic responsibilities towards their children, to the neglect of father-child relationships;
- and attempts to limit the working week have the potential to influence the quantity of father-child contact and the quality of family relationships.

Generally speaking the terms, conditions and expectations of paid employment stand as the greatest barrier to men's involvement in childcare.

C. Lewis, *A Man's Place in the Home: Fathers and families in the UK*, Joseph Rowntree Foundation, 2000

There are some signs of a more positive approach to 'family-friendly' policies from the current government, which are likely to prove supportive to fathers, although the steps so far have been relatively tentative. For example, from April 2003 fathers will be entitled for the first time to two weeks paternity leave, paid at £100 per week (or 90 per cent of average weekly earnings if this is less). Some new fathers on low incomes (those below the Lower Earnings Limit for National Insurance) would originally have been excluded from the scheme, but this anomaly has recently been rectified.

More broadly, the introduction of paid paternity leave sends an important signal to fathers that their participation in childcare is valued. Some argue, however, that the entitlement is too low, and few fathers will be able to take it up. The government has also announced the introduction of 13 weeks' parental leave for each child under five. Again, this sends a positive message, but there are severe doubts as to whether fathers will make use of this provision, particularly as it is unpaid (only an estimated two per cent of men take up parental leave currently, compared with a third of women workers). In both the case of paternity leave and of parental leave, it will be essential to ensure that targets for take-up by fathers are set, and progress towards them monitored. Experience in other European countries should also be taken into account. In Sweden, for example, where a strong tradition of gender equality has evolved, fathers have been encouraged to take parental leave by reserving one month of the overall year's leave specifically for them, which is lost if it is not used.[16]

For those in the lowest income categories, who are unable to find or sustain paid employment, measures such as paternity leave are irrelevant to their present situation. Measures such as the recent increases in levels of child benefit and the impending introduction of the child tax credit (see Chapter 4) are welcome. As lone parent fathers in a recent survey by Gingerbread argued, however, financial support is also needed to cover education-related costs for children (such as the costs of school uniforms and extra-curricula activities), to help smooth the transition into work, to reform the design and administration of Housing Benefit, to simplify the benefits system, and to improve services.[17]

Equally important are the intended reforms to the 1991 Child Support Act. The introduction of the controversial Child Support Agency in 1993 prompted a backlash from fathers' rights groups, arguing that the level of payments sought were exorbitant, and seeking to restore what they saw as an erosion of men's rights (especially in relation to child custody). As a result, in 1995 the system was reformed to reduce the amount that many absent fathers would have to pay. But the changes were complex and still produced results many claimed were anomalous. The government is therefore planning to reform the law again, introducing a simpler formula for deciding payments. Under the proposed system, those on incomes less than £100 per week have to pay a flat rate of £5, with a sliding scale where the income is between £100 and £200.[18] It remains to be seen what the impact of these new financial arrangements will be in practice.

Finally, the government has announced plans to give 'Parental Responsibility' automatically to fathers whose names are registered on the birth certificate. At present, when a child is born to married parents, both have legal powers in relation to issues such as deciding on the child's name, upbringing, education, medical treatment, and religion. If the parents are not married, however, Parental Responsibility is only awarded automatically to the mother, and the father must make a formal legal agreement with the mother to acquire Parental Responsibility. Research has shown that three-quarters of fathers are unaware of this difference in legal status, and almost all unmarried fathers believe the current law to be illogical, unfair, and out-of-date.[19]

Supporting fathers: the challenge for services

Fathers have a crucial role to play in their children's upbringing, and their involvement can be particularly important to their sons. Most voluntary and professional organisations currently working with parents acknowledge that it is much more difficult to encourage fathers to participate in parenting support than mothers. Some organisations have already developed programmes which specifically target fathers.

Home Office, 'Supporting Families: A consultation document', www.homeoffice.gov.uk/vcu/suppfam.htm, 1998

The government's Ministerial Group on the Family (co-ordinated by the Home Secretary) has stated in particular that it intends to improve the support available to fathers. Although there are some risks, enabling men to demonstrate their capacity to care is a challenge integral to the promotion of gender equality, and is likely to have significant benefits for children's development.

In practice child welfare services, whether formal or informal, have had little success so far in engaging with fathers, even though these services are potentially important sources of support, especially but not exclusively to those in vulnerable categories: unemployed fathers, young fathers, non-resident fathers, and stepfathers.

A central feature of all of these institutions is of course that they are 'gendered'. Although there have been many laudable attempts to alter the balance, the workers and users are almost always women. Service provision and policy design continue to draw heavily on the enduring ideological assumption that childcare is essentially women's work. As a result, the approach of services to engaging with men is also often ambivalent.

Although workers may express a wish that fathers should be more active in the care of their children, and more supportive to their female partners, in practice they often provide services that are predominantly geared to addressing women's needs. And while it is true that men may absent themselves from responsibility for childcare, it is also true that they may be 'screened out' by such ambivalence.[20]

In consequence, fathers are not only absent from discussions about the welfare of their children, but they are also absolved from responsibility. This places women under great pressure to take prime responsibility and be 'fit mothers'; meanwhile, workers routinely avoid assessing fathers by the same rigorous criteria, tending to see them in the role of supplementary carer, rather than co-parent. Redressing this balance so that services put in place identifiable strategies to include fathers is a critical task for policy, training, and practice.

Fathers Plus

Fathers Plus was started in 1997, initially as a three year project principally covering Tyne and Wear. The project now incorporates a wider area, with contacts from other regions. Its overall aim is 'to ensure that the role of father is valued, supported, and included in all approaches to working with children and families'. The project's objectives are:

- to develop, deliver, and disseminate effective practical approaches to parent-support for fathers;
- to co-ordinate the North East Forum (the network of colleagues committed to working with fathers) as a means of continually improving practice;
- through advocacy and empowerment, to ensure that the role of fathers is included in planning services for children and families.

Since May 2001 the remit of the project has broadened, with funding for part-time posts to cover direct work with fathers in seven Sure Start programmes across the region. The project manager works on an advisory and consultancy basis with other Sure Start projects, and has been actively involved in the training of teams and in their planning and delivery of services to fathers. In partnership with three Sure Start programmes, Fathers Plus has undertaken two major consultation exercises with fathers and male carers, leading to the informed development and delivery of 'fatherwork' in those areas. The model of consultation developed by Fathers Plus has now been adopted and used by other agencies and organisations within the region.

Support for colleagues trying to work inclusively with fathers in health, education, social services, and the voluntary sector takes place through the bi-monthly meetings of the North East Forum of Fathers Group workers. Sessions provide a training element as well as peer-support and information sharing. Group work with fathers has also taken place in other settings including youth offending teams, bail hostels, and prisons.

It is important to acknowledge that there are risks in involving fathers in childcare. Workers may rightly decide to avoid contact with a particular man, owing to the potential or actual extent of his violence or abuse towards his partner or children. There is also a related argument that the hidden and under-reported extent of male violence and abuse should place significant restrictions on the numbers of men employed as child-carers and the way in which they carry out their role.[21] However, a recent survey of the UK evidence suggests that issues of gender in childcare practice should be separated from issues of potential sexual abuse in early childhood services.[22] Whether male workers are being actively recruited or not, concerns about abuse must be clearly addressed within services and agencies, so that safeguards are in place to minimise risks and ensure that proper training, supervision, and support are readily available. More broadly, if the culture of child welfare institutions is based upon empowerment and openness, the potential for abuse will be minimised.

Another source of tension that inhibits male participation in services, either as users or workers, is that many women are wary that it may result in men taking over one of the few arenas – caring for children – in which women are able to exert some control over their lives. However, there is also a strong argument that perpetuation of the identification of women with children damages women's wider economic and social opportunities. If child-welfare services are to articulate gender roles positively, and thereby help to release women from being defined purely as the carers, they must engage with men more actively.

This is a tension that must be managed constructively. At service level, it may be that female users (and sometimes male users) will want to address some issues separately in single-sex groups, and such wishes should be taken into account. Within organisations as a whole, the corollary to attempts to increase men's participation as workers should surely be encouragement for women to enter senior management positions.[23]

> *At times I feel like a bloke turned up at a Women's Institute meeting.*
> Ian

> *Being a male member of a group, the women think you are only there to pick up women. Finding it very difficult to explain that's not what I want.*
> Thomas

> *Men tend not to share their problems or talk with friends ... it's up to fathers to forget their pride and get involved.*
> Jim

> *Local groups can help lone fathers and mothers get in touch with each other, to provide each other with support. Those in similar situations understand the pressures better.*
> Derek

Lone fathers quoted in *Becoming Visible: Focus on lone fathers*, Gingerbread, 2001

A final set of obstacles to male involvement is essentially practical. Long working hours or irregular employment patterns may preclude men's attendance at times when services are open. Services may also lack any 'father-friendly' orientation or 'feel'. For instance, the physical environment of posters, photographs, and information leaflets may not convey the message that men's participation is valued. The nature of the welcome given to male users may well affect their desire to come through the door again, and although having male workers may be useful, there is no firm evidence that their presence is seen as essential. Male attendees may also perceive the activities on offer as too passive, which leaves staff with the dilemma of how to attract men while seeking to challenge gender stereotypes.[24]

There are no easy solutions to this wide range of issues, and addressing and managing the tensions in engaging with men are primarily a matter of making gender visible within services. As recent research by Cameron *et al.* argues, it is vital to create opportunities for informed and on-going discussion and reflection among male and female workers and managers (and, where relevant, with service users of both sexes as well), in order to move forward on key matters of policy and practice.[25] Based on research he is currently conducting for the Home Office, Trefor Lloyd of Working With Men suggested that clearer evidence of what works with fathers was emerging from the initiatives which do exist. For him, key success factors are focusing on a positive approach to parenting, and a strong skills basis (that is, not only discussion, but also role play and practical parenting skills). As with protection strategies, if such approaches are to be successful, they require consistent backing from the agencies within which services are located.

Practical initiatives to support fathers

Although there is a lot of interest generally in fathers and their role in families and influence on children's development, in the past little was done by any of the childcare agencies to engage fathers and father figures ...

Future policy developments, for example those around early preventive services, should recognise the positive role that fathers can play in child development and should also recognise the lack of services which are father friendly or which encourage them to engage with the agencies providing services to their children.

M. Ryan, *Working With Fathers,* Department of Health, Radcliffe Medical Press, 2000

While increasing policy attention is being devoted to fathers, project development remains slow and hard to sustain (although it appears that more activity is being generated in the voluntary than the statutory sector). Adrienne Burgess, who in 1997 surveyed 44 organisations working with fathers for the Institute for Public Policy Research, argues that few of these programmes now survive. Mapping of services for parents currently being undertaken by the government-sponsored National Family and Parenting Institute apparently indicates similar results in relation to projects working with fathers.

Nevertheless, in 1999 the Home Office funded 16 projects to work exclusively with fathers and young men under the Family Support Grants, offering £1 million over a three-year period to do so. These projects include:

- DIY Dads, a project set up by Working With Men to compare and pilot different models of support for fathers;

- Fathers Direct;

- Dads and Lads programmes run by the YMCA;

- 'boys2MEN', a project run by the Thomas Coram Foundation, helping young black and ethnic minority care leavers to tackle issues concerning masculinity and fatherhood;

- research by Gingerbread into the needs of lone fathers for practical, emotional, and social support;[26]

- a range of model services specifically aimed at fathers, developed by NewPin, a national organisation offering programmes to parents under stress.

Welcome though such funding is, there was some scepticism among those interviewed by this study as to its impact and sustainability. Several pointed out that the funding runs out after three years. An IPPR publication on support groups for fathers has argued that:

> ... this recent financing of fathers' groups is not part of a long-term development strategy. The Home Office has not yet looked to integrate fathers' groups with the wider statutory and voluntary sectors, attempted to co-ordinate groups' work, or taken responsibility for the top-down promotion of father responsive family services. Funding 16 fathers' projects does not a 'father-friendly' family policy make.[27]

There are indications that the climate is changing, however. In particular, the introduction of the government's Sure Start programme, which aims to improve the life chances of 400,000 children under the age of four in disadvantaged areas by 2004, is apparently providing good opportunities to make a significant impact in developing 'fatherwork'.

Fathers Direct

Fathers Direct is the national information centre for fatherhood, funded by the Home Office to develop national quality standards for father-friendly services. It works to promote the well-being of children by harnessing the full potential of fathers to reduce delinquency and crime, raise educational achievement, improve health, and prevent child abuse. The Fathers Direct Network:

- provides training to health, family, and children's services on running effective services;
- works with other organisations to set up conferences on key issues;
- offers a consultancy service to organisations;
- manages an online database of father-friendly services (at www.fatherwork.org);
- publishes a quarterly magazine *FatherWork*, giving the latest news, views, research, and innovations for family-support agencies;
- publishes 'FatherFacts', summaries of latest research and key practice issues;
- runs a website for all fathers (www.fathersdirect.com).

Dads and Lads

The YMCA's Dads and Lads project was developed in response to the need for projects focusing exclusively on working with fathers or father figures. The scheme, developed by the YMCA and Care for the Family with funding from the Home Office, was launched in Plymouth in 1998 and has been extended to 30 projects nationwide, including with Liverpool and Leeds Football Clubs. Dads and Lads seeks to bring families closer together by giving fathers and sons the chance to play team sports, with the men having the opportunity to join a parenting course with other fathers. The projects organise sports sessions, providing valuable time together for fathers as well as building excellent memories for the boys. Sessions can be either weekly or monthly and last for a couple of hours. They can be followed up by a friendly chat after the game about the children and the challenges of parenting. To support the work, Care for the Family in conjunction with the YMCA has produced Dad, a men's magazine, which forms the basis of a ten-session course with the men.

The project has been very successful, as shown by these comments from a father on the Plymouth scheme:

My son had been going to the YMCA for years and he always came home from the club full of fun and excitement; anxious to tell me how many runs he had scored or how he had leapt six feet across the goal line to save a penalty in the last minute. I have to be honest and say that I wasn't really listening – despite caring, my mind was caught up with other matters; that little problem at work or which day to fit the car in for a service. He forced me to come along to Dads and Lads on the first session and we haven't looked back since. Our relation-ship has developed and deepened in a way which I never thought was possible. The YMCA has changed the whole of my family life. Spending time with my children is now a priority because I love to share in their laughter.

Based on an article by D. Uitterdijk, on the website of the National Family and Parenting Institute, www.nfpi.org/data/spotlight/lads_dads.htm

---

Beyond funding, questions remain about the values underpinning the work that is being undertaken. Ghate *et al.*, in their research into the work of 13 family centres with fathers, draw up three overall 'orientation' groupings for projects (similar to the framework suggested by Kabeer but with a less strong emphasis on the importance of coherent gender analysis, see Chapter 2):[28]

- 'gender-blind' centres, which tended to take the view that men should be treated exactly the same as women users, sometimes expressed in terms of an explicit policy of equal opportunities within the centre;
- 'gender-differentiated' centres, which tended to take the view that working with men presented different challenges to working with women, and both staff and users expressed views that stressed gender differences;
- 'agnostic' centres, which appeared not to have formulated an explicit view about whether working with fathers required a particular approach or not.

Ghate *et al.* conclude that 'at a basic level, having a strategy and a commitment to involving men is more important than what precise approach is taken to achieve this. Thus both "gender-blind" and "gender-differentiated" centres ... were doing better at getting men engaged at entry level than "agnostic" ones'.

How these orientations played out in practice was evident from the centres' priorities and policies (for example, in relation to their referral systems and attitudes to working with fathers); from the presence of male workers on the staff; from the activities provided (e.g. whether they included practical activities); and from the general atmosphere of the centre. Overall, it appeared that centres tended to take a different approach depending on the sex of the parent. Work with women tended to follow a family-focused model, in which women's needs were acknowledged as mothers and as women in their own right. On the other hand, work with fathers was more child-focused, with an emphasis on childcare and with little that catered to fathers' wider interests.

Interviewed for this research, Trefor Lloyd of Working With Men said he did not think that gender policies were particularly developed among fatherhood projects, though he cited the example of DIY Dads. The project statement below was drawn up based on the findings of a review of existing work in Lewisham in south London, together with a series of consultations with fathers, and is intended to underpin the development of all the project's activities. These are likely to include advice sessions, weekend nurseries, a domestic violence initiative targeting fathers, father-friendly services and 'Father's Day' activities, the development of fact sheets and booklets, and a Fatherhood in Schools programme.

DIY Dads

1. Most fathers want to be more involved with their children and may need support, opportunities to develop skills, and encouragement to do this.
2. Race, culture, religion, masculinities, and age all play a part in defining fatherhood for individual men.
3. Fathers are important to their children, and children important to their fathers.
4. Involved fathers result in happier families.
5. Fathers not living with their children are still important and can provide a valuable contribution to their children's lives.
6. Work, skills levels, and their perception of manhood can all be barriers to increasing fathers' involvement.
7. Public policy too often fails to support fathers in terms of parental leave, child support arrangements, divorce settlements, and the legal status of fathers.
8. While we are pro-fathers, this is not to the detriment of women and children. We will not support individual fathers' actions when they have a harmful effect on children and mothers (e.g. domestic violence and sexual abuse). However, we are very keen to support these fathers to change their abusive behaviours.

9. We believe that organisations such as DIY Dads are necessary, because of the recent and rapid changes in the roles taken by men and women, and not because 'women are now in charge', 'feminism has gone too far', or 'it is time for fathers to take back control of the family'.

DIY Dads, 'Underpinning principles, update', Working With Men, 2001

Developing models of support for low-income fathers

While there is widespread support for attempts to involve fathers more actively with their children, there are practical barriers for fathers, especially in disadvantaged groups. As outlined above, enduring cultural stereotypes of men as breadwinners result in policy being dominated by an economic view of fathering. As a result men's parenting is 'too often depicted as a social problem rather than a social strength'.[29] In fact, research is increasingly showing that the widely promoted image of 'feckless fathers' ignores the diversity of men's commitment to parenting. Research into the experiences of lone fathers, for instance, demonstrates that they have to confront and overcome issues such as negative stereotyping, inflexible workplaces, lack of support, and lack of skills in order to become more active parents – and many are successful in doing so.[30]

Even among young non-resident fathers, a group which is often vilified for irresponsible attitudes and behaviour, there are many who are willing and eager to engage in a responsible and caring relationship with their children, and do contribute to maintenance (although sometimes in the form of gifts, clothing, and childcare, rather than cash).

A range of issues can hinder men's involvement. As Speak *et al.* have argued, unmarried fathers are often unaware of their lack of legal rights in relation to their children.[31] Unemployment and the resulting lack of money also prevent men from being involved in the way that they want to be. The suitability of fathers' accommodation, and costs of transporting children to it, affects contact between children and their non-custodial parents. Speak *et al.* conclude, among other things, that:

- there is a need for a wide-reaching education programme to inform single fathers of their legal situation;

- fatherhood offers an opportunity to encourage young men into training, education, and employment. Lessons can be learned from work being carried out in the US, where fatherhood projects have been successful in encouraging men to re-enter education or employment for the sake of their children;

- access to affordable housing should be improved, and should be linked to a package of support, including training and support for fatherhood.

boys2MEN

boys2MEN aims to discover the extent to which young males in care are affected by the experience, and by the absence of their father or a positive male relationship. It seeks to devise a programme of intervention to enable 'looked after' boys and young men to become responsible individuals and committed fathers.

Alongside one-to-one support sessions, music and other art forms have been used to initiate group work, tackling sensitive subjects in a non-threatening way. To date, the project has worked with over 70 young men aged 14-19, referred by a variety of voluntary and statutory organisations across London. Eighty per cent of these attendees were from black minority ethnic groups and 20 per cent were teenage fathers.

The project believes it has had great success in engaging young men in care, many of whom are now working and preparing themselves for parenthood in a planned way, better equipped to live up to their responsibilities. All of the young fathers are more actively involved in the lives of their children. One participant commented that:

> *The discussions about fathers made me really angry. Sitting there listening just reminded me of him ... boys2MEN gave me the courage to go and see my dad for the first time ... I now know what he looks like ... I'm much calmer now and feel able to get on with my life.*

David, 19

Based on M.K. Davis, 'Preparing young men in care for fatherhood', article in *Working With Young Men*, Volume 1, January 2002

Summary

Growing numbers of women at work; rising divorce rates; declining marriage rates; increasing cohabitation: although factors such as these have undermined traditional notions of fathers as breadwinners and mothers as carers, these stereotypes still have a significant impact in practice. For many working fathers, long working hours adversely affect their ability to care for their children. For those in particular groups (such as fathers who are unemployed, young, cohabiting, non-resident, or stepfathers), the issues are different. Unemployed fathers, for example, are much more likely than other fathers to regard themselves as failed providers.

Child-welfare services do not engage very effectively with fathers, even though the former are potentially important sources of support (especially for those who are socially excluded). The evidence suggests that only a few are gender aware (mainly those in the voluntary sector), and even fewer (e.g. DIY Dads in Lewisham) have specific gender policies in place. Backed by Home Office funding, some fatherhood projects have emerged in recent years, but progress is slow and hard to sustain.

In practice, services tend to address women's needs primarily, and to devote less attention to encouraging men to attend. For instance, opening times may preclude men's attendance as they are at work, project environments may not feel father-friendly, and fathers may not be invited to key meetings relating to their children's health. While this ambivalence is understandable (due to fears of violence, or of men taking over 'women's space', for example), it is important that such services seek to engage more actively with fathers if they are to release women from being defined purely as carers.

Policy discussion in this area tends to be dominated by an economic view of fatherhood, with images of 'feckless fathers' predominant. Yet there is research evidence to suggest that many fathers (even among those who are young and socially excluded) are willing to contribute to their children's upbringing, and too often negative cultural images undermine the potential benefits of men's involvement. Moreover, they face significant practical barriers: lack of awareness of their rights; unemployment and lack of money; unsuitable accommodation for childcare; and costs in transporting children between two homes. While government policy has shifted towards a more supportive approach towards fatherhood (for example, by the introduction of parental leave and paid paternity leave), the evidence above suggests that further measures are necessary to address the full range of issues facing fathers who are poor or socially excluded.

9
Conclusions and recommendations

Gender inequality is preventing us from eliminating poverty. Gender equality should recognise both women's and men's needs, and how these interact. Usually women are at a disadvantage, but sometimes a special focus is needed on men and boys.

Department for International Development, 'Breaking the Barrier', Issues Paper, 1998

This study contacted 28 projects in England, Scotland, and Wales to assess the nature, scope, and effectiveness of work with men that impacts on poverty and social exclusion. A small-scale study of this kind cannot hope to do justice to the range of work that is going on across the UK. We believe, however, that our snapshot of projects working in the fields of employment training, men's health, violence and crime, and fatherhood (together with the materials arising from a consultation seminar held during the project) provides a solid basis for clear conclusions and recommendations about the direction that work with men should take if it is to have a positive impact on poverty and social exclusion.

This project draws largely upon the experiences of those working with men at grassroots level; hence our findings are geared primarily at the development of work at this level. While we make some recommendations that have broader policy, funding, or research implications, we do not seek here to define in detail a comprehensive agenda to be developed at national level. We believe this can only arise from a more systematic analysis of national policy than our project aimed to achieve.

Improving gender analysis

In Chapter 1, we identify that social research has in recent years developed increasingly complex and subtle theoretical approaches to men and masculinities, recognising for example that:

- there is no one universal pattern of masculinity (hence the use of 'masculinities');
- 'collective' masculinities can operate beyond the individual (e.g. within culture and institutions);
- masculinities are actively 'produced' by individuals, rather than being programmed by genes or fixed by social structures;
- masculinities are dynamic, changing according to specific historical circumstances.

In analysing a situation in order to assist project or programme development, the 'social relations' framework[1] explores the immediate, underlying, and structural factors that need to be addressed, and their effect on the various actors involved. It is then possible to consider what any intervention will be intended to achieve, how it will be approached, and how it will be evaluated. There are various approaches to developing gender analysis,[2] though Oxfam believes that the 'social relations' model is particularly helpful, as it provides a dynamic and holistic analysis of poverty, links what is happening at different institutional levels, and emphasises women's and men's different interests and needs.

Also useful is the way this model seeks to classify gender policies and practices into two basic types: 'gender-blind' and 'gender-aware'. Based on this approach, this study found that although some projects were set up specifically to address masculinity issues, many others were effectively gender-blind. In other words, the latter failed to make any distinction between the sexes, and thereby entrenched existing biases (often implicitly in favour of men). Although not universally the case, it appears that this orientation is especially widespread within the field of employment training, where projects are often designed and run along relatively traditional lines.

At the other end of the continuum, gender-aware approaches (those that recognise men and women as having differing and sometimes conflicting needs, interests, and priorities) were most developed among perpetrator projects working on sexual and domestic violence. The majority of these projects have detailed policy statements and minimum-practice standards in place. While some interviewees argued that the content of such statements was sometimes restrictive in focus and lacked flexibility, the existence of the policies and the efforts devoted to developing them is nevertheless impressive. By comparison, gender analysis does not often appear to translate to other project interventions to tackle men's violence.

One feature of projects working on domestic violence is that they usually pay particular attention to ensuring links with local projects working with women. These contacts appear to have bolstered the importance of gender analysis for the former. It seems likely that the gender perspective is most prominent in sexual and domestic violence because women's groups have demanded this. This suggests that efforts to improve links between projects working with men and projects working with women could prove beneficial in other sectors as well.

In addition, there was a range of projects set up to meet the targeted needs of men, but without specific gender statements. It was evident, nevertheless, that many of these projects had an intrinsic awareness of gender issues from the way the project was designed, implemented, and described by project staff, even though the particular approach adopted was not set out on paper. This was frequently, but not always, the case for men's health and fatherhood projects. Caution is necessary here, however; without a defined and agreed team or agency perspective, there is a danger that staff understanding and practice in relation to the complex issues involved in gender analysis can easily revert to traditional (and often male-biased) models.

A key finding of this study is therefore that it is essential to develop clear aims and objectives in order to work with men effectively.

Recommendations

- Gender-aware approaches, which take masculinities fully into account, should be put in place across all sectors, through the development of gender analysis and based on clear concepts, clear policy statements, objective setting, and ongoing monitoring and evaluation.
- Institutional changes should underpin the development of gender-aware approaches (for example, in relation to staff recruitment and training, the management of performance, resource allocation, and organisational culture).
- A practical guide to gender analysis should be developed for projects working with men in the UK. This should include: an explanation of what 'gender analysis' is; how it can be of benefit; how to undertake it; and how to respond in practice to the findings.

- Those working in sectors that appear to be relatively gender-blind (such as employment training) should learn from the experience of those in sectors where gender analysis has received greater attention.

- Regular contact should be established between local projects working primarily or exclusively with men, and projects working primarily or exclusively with women. The objective should be to exchange ideas and analysis, and develop a shared understanding of the needs of men and women in the area.

Mainstreaming masculinity and gender

Policy decisions that appear gender neutral may have a differential impact on women and men, even when such an effect was neither intended nor envisaged. Gender impact assessment is carried out to avoid unintended negative consequences and improve the quality and efficiency of policies.

European Commission, 'A Guide to Gender Impact Assessment', Office for Official Publications of the European Communities, 1998

The Global Platform for Action, adopted at the fourth World Conference on Women in Beijing in 1995, requests governments and other actors to mainstream a gender perspective into all policies and programmes. 'Mainstreaming' seeks to ensure that a gender dimension is integrated into all policy making, so that it takes account of gender inequality. It aims to assess policies for their adverse impact on women and men in order to develop appropriate responses. Focusing on equality of impact in this way represents a significant shift away from attempts to promote equality of treatment (e.g. through the introduction of laws to tackle sex discrimination), which have been criticised for failing to address the root causes of discrimination and to challenge the assumption that men are the norm.

Within the UK, gender mainstreaming is relatively undeveloped, especially at UK-government level (see Chapter 4). For instance, gender-impact assessment is only carried out systematically by the Department for International Development, and gender-disaggregated statistics are not routinely published by departments. Nevertheless, there is some evidence of recent attempts to pilot such analysis, both through the Women and Equality Unit and through other departments such as the Treasury.[3]

There is considerable experience to draw upon in this field, especially from initiatives at EU level, where the European Commission has taken a number of important steps to ensure that gender equality is integrated into policy making and other activities, (most recently issuing a Communication on a Community Framework Strategy on Gender Equality[4]). Some time ago, the EU also made gender mainstreaming a condition of receiving grants through the Structural Funds, owing to its long-standing emphasis on addressing gender inequalities in the labour market. Initiatives also exist at local government level in the UK[5] and within the Welsh Assembly, Scottish Executive, and Northern Ireland (see Chapter 4).

> The Government Statistical Service aims always to collect and make available statistics disaggregated by gender, except where considerations of practicality or cost outweigh the identified need. All GSS publications contain the name and contact details of a person who can explain which, if any, of the statistics are available by gender and how they can be obtained.
>
> *Hansard Written Answers*, 15 July 1998, col. 201-2

Several interviewees for this study commented that it was hard to get masculinities onto the agenda of larger institutions. Innovative approaches can be supported at project level (or via outsiders), but these may often be set within a wider organisational context which is gender-blind. Local initiatives are therefore inseparable from wider action to mainstream gender across institutions as a whole.

Interviewees in this study supported the development of gender main-streaming within agencies through the development of appropriate policies, implementation strategy, and regular monitoring and evaluation. However, the researchers discerned a degree of uneasiness among some interviewees as to the extent to which gender mainstreaming took masculinities into account. Indeed, it was occasionally suggested that gender mainstreaming is often (erroneously) regarded as synonymous with action to promote women's interests.

Recommendations

- Central government should devote greater attention to ensuring that gender is mainstreamed across all policy areas, building on existing initiatives and mechanisms. Such an approach should include the further development of gender-impact assessment and gender-disaggregated statistics, and a review of the effectiveness of current institutional arrangements.

- Further work is necessary to ensure that a focus on masculinities is integrated fully within any organisational initiatives to mainstream gender, building on innovative initiatives at EU, national, and local levels.

Targeting male poverty

Using key 'entry points'

While none of the projects approached stated that its aim was primarily to address poverty and social exclusion among men, the vast majority believed that poverty and social exclusion did form an important back-drop to their work, and that their interventions had some impact – either directly, or more often, indirectly – on addressing these issues.

The significance of poverty and social exclusion as a factor impacting on the work of programmes appeared to vary between sectors, however. Overall, projects working on men's health were able to draw upon a growing body of work, largely endorsed by government, which has identified the critical role of inequalities in influencing health outcomes for men and women, and for different categories of men. For these projects, therefore, tackling poverty and social exclusion was increasingly seen as central to their efforts.

In relation to employment, there is widespread professional and public support for the government mantra of recent years that getting a job is a key route out of poverty and social exclusion. Opinions appear to differ, however, as to whether it is the only route out; many believe that policy has over-emphasised efforts to find paid work, and devoted insufficient attention to the needs of those who are still likely to remain outside the labour market. Although the gendered nature of poverty and social exclusion seems to remain relatively invisible to many employment training projects, the fact that they have contact with large groups of unemployed men makes them a high-priority arena for tackling masculinity issues – especially given the significant resources being currently devoted to this area by government.

Over the past decade the issue of 'feckless' fathers has been a continuing source of concern to policy makers, and probably the main motor behind the steady, if haphazard, growth in the number of fatherhood projects in existence. While 'fatherlessness' has been repeatedly blamed for fuelling a range of social problems, including juvenile delinquency, crime, violence, and unemployment, there is evidence to suggest that the main underlying problem is not father absence *per se*, but the poverty and social exclusion which many families face. Fatherhood projects therefore do provide an important opening for tackling poverty among disadvantaged men.

As with employment projects, those tackling violence (and other criminal justice projects) also work with a very high proportion of men, the vast majority young and working class. It is therefore somewhat surprising that masculinity issues do not appear to be consistently addressed by practitioners. This may be in part the result of the relative dominance of cognitive reasoning approaches (within probation services, for example), which seek to change the offender's individual thinking patterns, rather than address broad social factors. The only area where masculinity is a central focus appears to be in the small number of domestic violence projects, where the predominant approach is to challenge the offender to accept responsibility for his actions. Many of these projects do not believe that poverty and social exclusion are important factors in causing the offending in the first place, arguing that their clients are by no means exclusively from working class backgrounds. Be this as it may, it seems odd that among the full range of project work carried out with offenders, attention to masculinity and to 'men as men' is so muted. In our view, this could and should be an area for development.

A major conclusion of this study is therefore that health, employment, fatherhood, and violence projects are all, actually or potentially, significant entry points for tackling men's poverty and social exclusion. As we have argued above, however, the extent to which poverty and social exclusion can be addressed varies from sector to sector. Beyond the specific sectoral entry point, it is clear from the descriptions of several project staff that their work frequently touched upon deep-seated anxieties related to masculinity, such as men's fear of failure, lack of self-esteem, isolation, emotional closure, and stereotypical assumptions about gender. This finding suggests that attempts to tackle these issues (e.g. by building self-awareness and self-esteem) can have important knock-on effects on men's ability to respond positively to the challenge presented by the project.

Recommendation

• In order to tackle poverty and social exclusion among men, policy makers, professionals, and funders should seek to develop innovative work on masculinities via key entry points, including health, employment training, and fatherhood projects. Further exploration of the potential of projects that tackle violence to address poverty and social exclusion is also necessary.

Encouraging cross-sectoral linkages

One striking finding from this study was the lack of connection between different sectors working with men, and the failure to acknowledge the potential benefits of improving such links. For instance, although schemes such as New Deal address a range of issues facing participants (such as job search, careers advice, and financial help), it appears that they are generally less able to assist with 'personal' issues, including deep-seated attitudes to masculinity. Yet these latter factors can be crucial in the success or failure of a programme for the individual. As Fothergill *et al.* argue: 'The implications of change in family circumstances, and, to a lesser extent, of change in gender roles, are rarely appreciated as relevant to policy on male labour force attachment and employability, yet they are clearly critical factors in some cases'.[6]

The impact of poor mental and physical health on the ability of individual men to seek work is also significant, yet a focus on these issues within employment training is virtually absent. Attempts are lacking to transfer some of the positive communication strategies developed in relation to young men's health (see CALM, Chapter 6) to the field of employment.

Beyond the labour market, it was suggested to the researchers during this study that services working with fathers should build more links with other services relevant to them such as housing, employment, and financial advice. In particular, there appears to be a role for fatherhood projects to link more closely with services to address problems around mental health, alcohol and drug misuse, and relationships.[7]

While some positive cross-sectoral work was evident in this study (for example, Let's Get Serious, Manchester), we conclude that this was far too seldom the case. Several interviewees mentioned that they were aware that practice in the US was far more advanced in this respect, citing projects, for example, linking fatherhood with work on health, and employment with fatherhood. Exploring the wide variety of welfare approaches adopted in Europe is also likely to be worthwhile, especially in light of increasing efforts to tackle poverty and social exclusion.

Recommendations

- Greater efforts should be made both at national and local levels to encourage cross-sectoral links and the sharing of good practice between those working with men. This should include a stronger lead from government, more innovative approaches to funding partnerships bringing together different sectors, and the development of joint training and support networks between local projects.

- Further research is required to explore the extent, nature, and values of programmes in the USA and mainland Europe which link together different sectors (e.g. around fatherhood and work), and how far they may be transferable to the UK.

Making masculinities visible

Responding to diversity

Black men often cope with their frustration, embitterment and alienation and social impotence by channelling their creative energies into the construction of unique, expressive and conspicuous styles of demeanour, speech, gesture, clothing, hairstyle, walk, stance and handshake.

R. Majors, 'Cool Pose: Black masculinity and sports', in
M. Messner and D. Sabo (eds.), *Sport, Men and the Gender Order*,
Human Kinetics Books, 1990

Addressing the full range of masculinities means looking beyond gender as the only factor defining difference. While we identify below in some detail the impact of age on how working class men experience their lives, it is also essential to explore the intersections of other aspects of masculinity (e.g. identity and race, disability, and sexual orientation) with social class.

Despite the undoubted importance of these issues, the evidence suggests that they have generally received limited research attention (although individual studies exist in some areas). For example, the recent Office of

National Statistics publication *Social Focus on Men* addresses social class to some extent, but provides little information on the circumstances of men from ethnic minorities, or those with disabilities (although health is covered more fully), and even less in relation to sexual orientation. Overall, we concur with Lloyd and Forrest in their review of men's health research that '... too often, studies appear to be unable to take into account more than one variable, so if they address age, then gender, race and other significant variables retreat into the background.'[8]

The interviews conducted for this study indicated that many projects did not make any particular efforts to address diverse masculinities, although some were clear that they were seeking to target specific groups of young men (e.g. the LEAP project's work with Afro-Caribbean men). This lack of awareness can also mean that masculinities remain invisible for specific groups across significant areas of work. For instance, the Social Exclusion Unit's report on *Rough Sleepers* identifies that 90 per cent of those sleeping rough are male, but then fails to explore the implications of this for the development of policy and practice.[9] In addition, while most UK asylum seekers are young single men (even though globally 80 per cent of refugees are women and children), the important masculinity issues involved (around isolation, loss of the breadwinner role, violence, and poverty, for example), have as yet been almost completely ignored.

> Most of the men talked about not being in control, having no purpose in life (if they couldn't work), empty days, isolated, the humiliation of the voucher system ...
>
> Working With Men, ' Project proposal for 18-30 males project at the Ethiopian Advice and Support Centre' (unpublished), John Lyon's Charity, 2001

Recommendations

- The individual needs of men must be recognised and responded to, rather than treating them as a homogenous group. In particular, this means that policy makers and professionals must take into account the relationship between masculinity and other issues such as social class, identity and race, disability, and sexual orientation. Further research is required to identify the most appropriate and effective learning strategies for different communities of men.

- Efforts should be strengthened at all levels to address the importance of masculinity issues for particular groups of men facing poverty

and disadvantage. This includes, for example, meeting the needs
of rough sleepers, asylum seekers and refugees, and disabled men.

Moving beyond young men as 'problem'

*The most essential factor ... was the nature of the relationships developed
with the young men. Young men engaged with the material, the subject
matter and us, and we engaged with the young men, full stop.*

T. Lloyd, 'Boys and young men 'Into Work' programme',
Working With Young Men, Volume 1, January 2002

Our research revealed considerable evidence of widespread anxiety among
and between men – especially young men at the sharp end of economic
and social change – as to their roles and their futures. In line with
Connell's theory of 'hegemonic masculinity' (see Chapter 2), this experience
can sometimes translate into aggressive attempts to shore up traditional
notions of masculinity by the reassertion of male power over, for example,
other marginalised men, women, ethnic minority groups, and gay men.

There is a long-standing British tradition of 'respectable fears' of lawless,
violent young men whose behaviour is seen as a threat to social order.[10]
There is also considerable evidence that the behaviour of young Afro-
Caribbean men is seen to be even more readily defined as 'problematic',
and in need of intervention to control it, than that of their white
counterparts – even though these groups have very similar rates of
offending. Against this background, there is a danger that repeated calls
from politicians and the media to 'crack down' on young men will be
counter-productive. As increasingly controlling measures are introduced,
young men will become more and more segregated and alienated from
mainstream society, and even more likely to respond with defiance.

Recent research by Frosch, Phoenix, and Pattman suggests the reality of
young men's lives indicates that a rather different approach may be more
fruitful. Many young men struggle to find ways of differentiating themselves from the 'hegemonic' codes of 'macho' masculinities, especially as
a result of pressure by peers and adults which communicates the message
to them that alternative 'softer' ways of being are 'abnormal for males –
that they are girlish and hence subject to opprobrium and exclusion'.[11]
In fact, this narrowness of conventional masculinities is a cause of
considerable bullying and teasing, and can lead to some men acting out
delinquency in response. The researchers conclude that young men can

be emotionally and intellectually articulate, thoughtful, and insightful, and need to be provided with close and supportive relationships which allow them to demonstrate these qualities.

The experience of those interviewed for this study suggests that if policy and practice are to have an impact on the attitudes and behaviour of young men, it is essential to develop an understanding of the centrality of masculinity issues in their lives. It is vital to adopt approaches which value the potential of young men to contribute to society, rather than simply treat them as a problem. As Davidson has written: '... an attitude of "positive regard" for young men is vital in developing work (especially when dealing with difficult behaviour). An absence of such a perspective is particularly likely to have consequences for the large numbers of young men who make tentative initial contact with agencies but then lose touch'.[12]

Recommendations

- If effective work is to be done with young men (especially those who are hard to reach), it is essential for policy makers and professionals to move beyond a perspective that sees their attitudes and behaviour purely as a problem.

- It is important for workers to engage with young men in a manner appropriate to their age and developing maturity, and to address seriously the issues that young men themselves raise. Projects that are supportive towards young men and relevant to their needs appear, unsurprisingly, to elicit more positive responses from them.

- Educational approaches to young men need to encompass both basic skills and personal and social skills (that is, not only reading, writing, and communicating, but also self-awareness, making decisions, handling conflict and authority, thinking for oneself, coping with feelings, handling relationships, and asking for help and support). Young men often appear to prefer structured and formal programmes, with some flexibility to respond to individual needs, rather than relatively unstructured programmes.

- Policy and practice should not focus too heavily on control and coercion, as this can fuel young men's resistance, but should also recognise young men's potential to contribute to society, and should assist them to do so. It is acknowledged that there are some instances (e.g. some work with serious offenders) where court requirements to attend may provide a necessary mandate for intervention.

Supporting older men more actively

It is vital that programmes for unemployed men, especially those who have been made redundant after working for many years, are not perceived to be punitive or based on insulting assumptions about their skills and lack of 'employability'. Those who formerly worked in traditional industries such as mining are highly skilled. Moreover there can be a chronic shortage of alternative jobs in the areas where male-dominated industries have been destroyed. If programmes for the unemployed do not take account of the harsh realities of the labour market, particularly in some of the most depressed industrial areas, they simply heighten feelings of depression, distrust and cynicism.

V. McGivney, 'Excluded Men: Men who are missing from education and training', NIACE, 1999

Focusing on young men as a 'problem' also has the effect of downgrading the needs of older men. The material collected for this study showed clearly that the attention of policy makers, researchers, and practitioners (and the funding which flows from this attention) is directed more frequently at addressing the needs of younger men. Rather than respond aggressively to the difficult economic and social conditions many working class men often face, it appears that older men are more likely to be prone to quiescent acceptance of their marginalisation. This can lead to a retreat from social networks and the labour market, and at worst mental and physical illness.

In our view, it is time that the issues facing older men received greater consideration from all key stakeholders. It is important to tackle some of the barriers that result in older men, particularly those who have been made redundant, becoming detached for a long period from the labour market. Programmes such as the New Deal for the Long-Term Unemployed and New Deal 50plus have a role to play, especially via the assignment of a personal adviser to every participant. It appears, however, that as yet there are substantial differences in the extent to which people feel that advisers understand, and respond to, their full range of needs.[13]

Recommendations

- Policy makers and professionals should seek to address the needs of older working class men in a more coherent way, both by extending the understanding of existing services (e.g. through the New Deal personal adviser system) and by developing particular initiatives to respond to their circumstances and concerns.

Alongside core elements of existing programmes, such as careers guidance and job-search skills, greater attention should be paid to financial and debt counselling, practical work experience, exercises in confidence building, and the development of computer-based learning.

- Too great a reliance on compulsion may prove counter-productive with older men, producing a truculent workforce, higher drop-out rates, and inhibiting more constructive relationships with personal advisers.

Promoting good practice in working with men

Attractive environments

Many workers, across a range of settings, report difficulties in attracting men to use services. Most importantly, recruitment strategies need to be sensitive. For example, advertising 'men's projects' can be perceived as threatening to some men. And although men's groups have proven successful on occasions (e.g. at 42nd Street in Manchester[14]), they are relatively small in number, and often hard to sustain.

Experience in the field of men's health suggests that it is often essential to do outreach work in the places where men go, as in the case of the Pilot project in Pubs in the West Midlands running health sessions for men (see Chapter 6). Alternatively, family centres sometimes report that men are willing to respond to home visits, but unwilling to visit centres, which they regard as 'women's places'. This is usually due to the fact that centres tend to have a predominantly female workforce and user group, and lack a 'father-friendly' orientation or environment.

It is essential to address the agendas of the men themselves, and to use language with which they are familiar. Young men in particular appear to value an element of humour as a tool to defuse situations or discussions that could otherwise be perceived as threatening. Particularly noteworthy in this respect is the communication strategy developed by CALM (The Campaign Against Living Miserably), which has used a range of approaches to successfully 'market' positive mental health among young men.

Persuading young men to do, think or believe anything is big business. Giants of industry in drinks brands, clothing labels and audio-visual equipment spend millions every year trying to do just that. But young men are no easy target – even for the multinationals. Arguably the advertising industry's most difficult client, young men don't follow patterns of behaviour as are more easily predicted of other audiences, and appealing to them with a 'product' is a fast moving, ever changing challenge. Yet this is the challenge we must rise to, and capture the attention of young men with a fraction of the budget and a far less sexy 'product': in essence, positive mental health.

Pippa Sargent, CALM, *Working With Young Men*, Volume 1, January 2002

Several interviewees for this study indicated the importance of a strong skills basis to the approach used (e.g. role play and practical parenting skills, rather than just discussion). It appears that in practice many men often do not regard talking as part of learning, though it is more possible to engage them through activities.

Consideration also needs to be given to the importance of the difference between 'public' and 'private' for men. Many men, especially within the younger age groups, learn early on how to develop a front to protect themselves in public settings from any threats to their masculinity. As Trefor Lloyd of Working With Men comments, the implications of this are that: '... if young men feel they are in a "public" environment, they are much less likely to talk openly and honestly, and are very unlikely to show their vulnerability. Alternatively, when young men think they are in a "private" environment, they are much more likely to talk openly and honestly, and are much more prepared to be vulnerable'.[15] One of the primary tasks for workers is therefore to create environments where the pressures for men to prove themselves or to maintain the front are minimal or non-existent.

Recommendations

- In order to attract men to use services, it is important to pay attention to developing appropriate communication strategies. These may include: eye-catching contemporary design and branding for materials and adverts; posting information in settings where men gather (such as job centres, sports centres, youth clubs); exploiting the potential of local radio, youth TV, and the Internet; and encouraging the involvement of positive role models from the worlds of music, sport, and entertainment. In some cases, men themselves may best communicate the benefits of particular services among their peers.

- Although there is a danger of perpetrating gender stereotypes, engaging men via recreational activities or technical skills training (e.g. photography, IT) can be an effective way in to working with them.

- Services should seek to work with men in settings which are easily accessible and within which they feel comfortable. This may mean outreach work and home visits are necessary, and attention to making men feel welcome in environments where women predominate.

- Working effectively with men involves addressing the issues that men feel are important to them, using language that resonates with them. A variety of methods can be successful, however men often appear to find practical skills training more accessible and useful than discussion.

- For many men, individual approaches – including mentoring and personal advisers – have an important role to play in encouraging them to be open with workers about more personal and private issues in their lives.

Developing professional attitudes

The evidence from a range of health and welfare services suggests that some professionals, either consciously or unconsciously, in practice exclude men from their services. For example, family services often focus primarily on the needs of mothers and children, thereby reinforcing the centrality of childcare as 'women's work' and defining men out of the equation.[16] Similarly, health services frequently fail to engage with many men, who feel that what is on offer is not designed for them.

Professional reluctance to engage with men arises for a range of reasons, including lack of confidence in communicating with men, lack of awareness of the issues facing men, and some concerns about working with them. Men themselves can also contribute to their exclusion, however. As Ryan writes, in relation to family services: 'Partly this is because professionals do not attempt to find out about or engage with fathers, partly it is because fathers distance themselves.'[17] The fact that men are often unwilling, or too embarrassed to attend a particular service, or may simply be unaware of what is on offer, needs also to be addressed.

We believe that greater efforts should be made by professionals to engage with men far more systematically. Although there may be occasions when individual assessment suggests that engagement could be counter-productive (if the man has a history of violence, for example), such cases should be treated as the exception rather than the norm.

Recommendation

- In order for professionals to respond more effectively to men, it is essential to make gender visible within services. This involves providing continuing opportunities for male and female staff to explore the gendered nature of the work they do, to develop agreed policies, and to reflect upon their practice. [18]

Promoting male participation at project level

Some interviewees suggested to the researchers that the presence of male project workers recruited locally and known to men in the community can be effective, both in terms of recruitment and of good project practice. Although having male workers may be helpful, there is no firm evidence that their presence is essential. One recent study suggested that for young men, it was an enthusiastic and positive approach which was highly valued, whether from a male or female worker.[19]

In the field of childcare, for example, there is research evidence to support the idea of men working with children, though the picture painted is not a straightforward one. According Cameron *et al.*, female carers tend to see themselves as professional role models, whereas there is lack of clarity about what kinds of role models male carers are intended to present.[20] They also suggest that employing isolated male workers is unlikely to make an impact on the number of fathers attending centres 'without a more structural and wide-ranging approach to gender issues within the centre's practice'.

This finding accords with the earlier suggestion of the present study that gender policies need to be given higher priority within projects. Related to this is the importance of developing overall strategies for increasing male participation that go beyond the needs of the individual project. Co-operation between the various local authorities, organisations, and institutions responsible is vital if appropriate policies and action plans are to be formulated and implemented.[21]

Another significant issue is the difficulty of employing male project workers with the right skills. It appears that often the relatively low pay levels and the related perception that caring is 'women's work' discourages them. And when they are taken on, they tend to move away from direct work (and frequently into management) relatively swiftly.

It has been suggested that changing employment trends may encourage more men into caring work as more jobs are created in the service sector.[22] This may not prove a straightforward transition, however: opposition was widespread to plans for considerable numbers of young men to train as child carers under the New Deal programme. Nevertheless, the DfEE suggested that 'the recruitment of men into the childcare workforce should also be actively encouraged; we need to establish a larger mixed gender-based workforce.'[23] It has set a target that six per cent of the child-care workforce should be male.[24] While this is a low figure – especially when compared to the target of 20 per cent recommended several years ago by the European Commission Network on Childcare[25] – the introduction of a target can in itself be viewed as a positive innovation.

Recommendations

- The presence of male workers with strong connections to the local areas in which they work helps to improve recruitment of male users and positive practice, however it is not essential. More important are attempts to make gender analysis more central to the work of all services through the ongoing development of policy, training, and monitoring.
- A clear gender analysis should be set within a co-ordinated strategy for promoting male participation which involves all the key stake-holders, including local authorities, voluntary organisations, individual projects, trade unions, employers, parents' organisations, and training providers.

Increasing funding for work on masculinity issues

Throughout this study, interviewees raised fears regarding the lack of funding for work with men. Several stated, for example, that the amount of money available from the Home Office to support fatherhood projects was relatively small. This view was not universal, however, and more than one respondent felt that the climate had changed, and that it was far easier nowadays to obtain funding for fatherhood or men's health projects than formerly. Comparing the amounts of government funding available to New Deal programmes targeted primarily at men and at women (see Rake, Chapter 4) suggests that men do relatively well overall.

The situation is also paradoxical: although New Deal programmes are relatively well funded, this study has shown that masculinity issues remain almost completely invisible within the central design and local implementation of projects. Moreover, beyond the labour market, there appears to be an insufficient number of support services and networks for men. In practice, projects that focus on fatherhood, men's health, and domestic violence make far more significant attempts to tap into and to respond to male experience, yet they are often surviving on far more limited and insecure funding bases. A survey by Lloyd and Forrest of 41 projects working with boys and young men recently concluded that 23 of them (56 per cent) were less than two years old. This is significant, as the evidence suggests that services often need to become well established and trusted before men will use them.[26]

We suggest that the funding position mirrors long-standing perceptions of what may be appropriate approaches to men and women among policy makers and funders (especially those within government). In relation to funding projects working with men, although a range of factors may be at play, there appears to be an underlying emphasis on shoring up and revitalising their breadwinner status. While this is significant for many men, we believe that accompanying attempts to assist them to explore the centrality of masculinity issues in their lives would also be worthwhile. Too often the latter initiatives may be seen as too 'soft' to be useful, or lacking in effective policy outcomes.

Recommendations

- Policy makers and funders should seek to devote fair and equitable resources to innovative projects working with men, in particular those which are seeking to address masculinity issues directly.
- It is essential that work with men should not divert significant resources from projects that work with women; men and women should work together to raise the profile of work on gender, and to seek to expand the overall level of funding available for such work.
- Attention must be devoted to ensuring that new initiatives are made sustainable, and lessons learned integrated into mainstream programmes and policies.

Taking forward the research agenda

This small-scale study has identified a range of areas for further research. In recent years, academic research has increasingly focused on masculinity issues and a range of projects have been undertaken in Britain in relation in particular to male violence, men and work, transitions to adulthood, and fatherhood. Reflecting this emphasis, in 2001 the Office for National Statistics has, for the first time ever, published *Social Focus on Men*, which provides a statistical picture of the experiences and lifestyles of men in the UK.[27]

The establishment of a Gender Research Forum (a collaboration between the Women and Equality Unit, Economic and Social Research Council, and Office for National Statistics) is also intended to encourage dialogue between researchers and policy makers in this field. The Office for National Statistics has recently announced a review of gender-disaggregated statistics (as part of a wider programme on equal opportunity statistics), and it is to be hoped that this will hasten the production of more comprehensive information in this area.

Despite this growing interest, our evidence suggests that some significant areas require further work. As we identify above, for example, much attention focuses on young men, whereas the difficulties facing older men are often ignored. Race, class, disability, and sexual orientation – and the intersections between diverse masculinities such as these and gender – require further study. Critical information is also lacking in relation to certain issues; for instance, social and economic statistics rarely distinguish between men who are and who are not fathers, whereas comparable statistics on women often reveal whether or not they are mothers, how many children they have, and how old their children are.[28] Pringle highlights that the existing research often displays a simplistic conceptual separation of the social problems which some men create, from the social problems which some men experience. He suggests that 'these connections and intersections should also be a major target for future research'.[29]

This study found that relatively little work had been done to map existing service provision in relation to work with men. Although some mapping is now under way (e.g. a National Family and Parenting Institute study of parenting services), further studies would flesh out the picture we present. Furthermore, few projects have carried out evaluations of their work, so a thorough analysis to establish the factors that encourage effective intervention is lacking. Attempts to explore and disseminate good project practice are relatively rare too (although exceptions exist, such as the work of the Working With Men consultancy), and this reinforces the isolation and lack of confidence that some projects feel in their work with men.

From the interviews for this study, the researchers gained a strong impression that those who are directly involved in working with men are sceptical as to the accessibility and applicability of some of the academic research which has been done. This is disappointing, given that much of this work should assist those working at the grassroots to develop more coherent gender analyses to inform their practice.

Based on his experience of the Nordic welfare tradition of promoting gender equality, Holter's analysis helps to explain why this disconnection is increasingly occurring.[30] He believes that: '... if one only highlights the problem of men or the need to monitor men's studies, probably most men will keep their absence and stay away'. He suggests that studies which are not just about men but also for men (that is, which address their self-development and are solution-orientated) are likely to have the most effect in moving men's practices in more positive directions. There are risks involved which must be avoided, in particular the danger of resurrecting backward looking 'men's rights' ideologies. There appears to be a strong feeling among practitioners, however, that if progress is to be made in working with men, then a continuing focus purely on 'men as problem' must be balanced by attempts to create a more positive, forward looking dialogue with men.

Recommendations

- The impact of masculinity issues for some disadvantaged groups of men (e.g. older men, ethnic minorities, refugees and asylum-seekers, homeless men, disabled men) has received little research consideration so far. Further attention should be directed at their particular circumstances and needs, so that appropriate pilot projects can be developed in response.

- One gap in the academic literature on men has been a lack of attention to the impact of different cultural contexts of Scotland, Northern Ireland, Wales, and England on the framing of masculinities.

- Further research is necessary to map services working with men across a range of sectors, to improve the number and quality of external evaluations of project work, and to explore and disseminate good practice in working with men.

- There are some fears that some critical research on men and masculinities is not accessible to practitioners and focuses too strongly on 'men as problem'. Closer relationships should be developed between academics and practitioners in this field in order to begin to bridge this gap and to develop more positive solution-orientated research.

Notes

Chapter 1

1 **F. Porter, I. Smyth, C. Sweetman** (1999) *Gender Works: Oxfam Experience in Policy and Practice*, Oxford: Oxfam GB

2 **C. March, I. Smyth, M. Mukhopadhyay** (1999) *A Guide to Gender-Analysis Frameworks*, Oxford: Oxfam GB

3 **UNPFA** (2000) 'Women's Empowerment and Reproductive Health: Links through the life cycle', www.unfpa.org/modules/intercenter/cycle/index.htm

4 The overall purpose of the UKPP is to have a direct impact on poverty and social exclusion in the UK, by strengthening the skills and capacities of the community and voluntary sector to tackle poverty more effectively, and by direct lobbying and campaigning based on Oxfam's domestic and international programme experience.

5 **N. May** (1997) *Challenging Assumptions: Gender Considerations in Urban Regeneration*, Joseph Rowntree Foundation in association with Oxfam GB

6 Various classifications are used to define social class. For the purpose of this research, Oxfam interprets 'working class' according to the broadly understood Registrar General's Social Scale, which identifies social class based on occupation. Under this classification, used by government statisticians until recently, the 'working class' would probably be identified as those in classes IIIM ('skilled manual'), IV ('partly skilled'), and V ('unskilled). It should be noted that the Social Scale has recently been replaced by the National Statistics Socio-economic Classifications, which sets out eight categories.

7 For Oxfam, 'gender equality' means moving beyond constricting notions of masculinity and femininity, and opens up a broader and richer set of options for how women and men work, behave, think, feel, and relate to one another. Oxfam believes that 'gender equality' is a more precise and measurable term than 'gender equity', especially in legal terms, and therefore more useful as a target to aim for, and for holding governments to account.

Chapter 2

1 **J. Scourfield, M. Drakeford** (2001) *New Labour and the Politics of Masculinity*, Paper 13, Working Paper Series, School of Social Sciences, Cardiff University

2 **Equal Opportunities Commission** (2001) *Sex Equality in the 21st Century*, Manchester: Equal Opportunities Commission

3 **Office for National Statistics**, News Release on *Social Focus on Men*, 12 July 2001

4 **Equal Opportunities Commission** (2002) *Facts About Women and Men in Great Britain*, Manchester: EOC

5 **D. Grimshaw, J. Rubery** (2001) *The Gender Pay Gap: A Research Review*, EOC Research Discussion Series, Manchester: EOC

6 **R. Connell** (1995) *Masculinities*, Cambridge: Polity

7 **A. Cornwall** (1997) 'Men, masculinity and "gender and development"' in **C. Sweetman** (ed.), *Gender and Development 5(2): Men and Masculinity*, Oxford: Oxfam GB

8 The UK Government increasingly uses a 60 per cent of median (mid-point) figure.

9 **D. Gordon, L. Adelman, K. Ashworth, J. Bradshaw, R. Levitas, S. Middleton, C. Pantazis, D. Patsios, S. Payne, P. Townsend, J. Williams** (2000) *Poverty and Social Exclusion in Britain*, York: Joseph Rowntree Foundation

10 'Employees in professional occupations: by gender', Labour Force Survey, Office for National Statistics, 2001

11 'Median gross and disposable individual income: by gender and age', New Earnings Survey, Office for National Statistics, 2001

12 'Men of working age: by employment status', Labour Force Survey, Office for National Statistics, 2001

13 'Male unemployment rates: by age', Labour Force Survey, Office for National Statistics, 2001

14 *Ibid.*

15 'Economic activity rates of men: by ethnic group and age', Labour Force Survey, Office for National Statistics, 2001

16 'Life expectancy of men: by social class, 1972-96', Longtitudinal Study, Office for National Statistics

17 *Independent Inquiry into Inequalities in Health* (1998), London: The Stationery Office

18 'Death rates among men: by age, 1971-99', Office for National Statistics; General Register Office for Scotland; Northern Ireland Statistics and Research Agency

19 'Main causes of death among men: by age, 1999', Office for National Statistics; General Register Office for Scotland; Northern Ireland Statistics and Research Agency

20 '1997 Mortality Statistics', Office for National Statistics (1999), London: The Stationery Office

21 'Prevalence of treated coronary heart disease among men: by age', Office for National Statistics, from Medicines Control Agency data,1998

22 'Prevalence of cigarette smoking among men, 1974-1999', General Household Survey, Office for National Statistics

23 'Percentage of adults drinking over specified levels of alcohol: by gender and age, 1998-99', General Household Survey, Office for National Statistics; Continuous Household Survey, Northern Ireland Statistics and Research Agency

24 'Body mass among men, 1993 and 1999', Health Survey for England, Department of Health

25 'Offenders as a percentage of the population: by gender and age, 2001', Criminal Statistics, Home Office

26 'Male offenders found guilty of, or cautioned for, indictable offences: by type of offence and age, 2001', Criminal Statistics, Home Office

27 **C. Kershaw, T. Budd, G. Kinshott, J. Mattinson, P. Mayhew, A. Myhill** (2000) *The 2000 British Crime Survey England and Wales*, London: Home Office

28 **A. Clancy, M. Hough, R. Aust, C. Kershaw** (2001) *Crime, policing and justice: the experiences of ethnic minorities*, findings from the 2000 British Crime Survey, HORS 223, London: Home Office

29 'Understanding and Responding to Hate Crime' (2001), A joint project funded by the Home Office Targeted Policing Initiative – Homophobic Violence fact sheet, London: Metropolitan Police

30 'Employment by family type 2001', Labour Force Survey, Office for National Statistics

31 'Time use: by gender, 1999', Omnibus Survey, Office for National Statistics

32 **J. Bradshaw, C. Stimson, C. Skinner, J. Williams** (1999) *Absent Fathers*, London: Routledge

33 **L. Segal** (1999) *Why Feminism?*, Cambridge: Polity

34 **S. Chant, M. Gutmann** (2000) *Mainstreaming Men into Gender and Development*, Oxfam Working Paper, Oxford: Oxfam GB

35 **R. Bly** (1990) *Iron John*, Reading, MA: Perseus Books

36 **J. Gray** (1993) *Men are from Mars and Women are from Venus*, London: Harper Collins

37 **M. Kimmel** (2000) *The Gendered Society*, New York: Oxford University Press

38 See for instance, **A. Cornwall, N. Lindisfarne** (eds.) (1994) *Dislocating Masculinity: Comparative Ethnographies*, London: Routledge

39 **T. Sewell** (1997) *Black Masculinities and Schooling: How Black Boys Survive Modern Schooling*, Stoke on Trent: Trentham Books

40 See for instance, **C. Cockburn** (1983) *Brothers: Male Dominance and Technological Change*, London: Pluto Press

41 **S. Frosh, A. Phoenix, R. Pattman** (2002) *Young Masculinities: Understanding boys in contemporary society*, Basingstoke: Palgrave

42 **J. Hearn** (1996) 'Is Masculinity Dead? A Critique of the Concept of Masculinity/masculinities', in **M. Mac an Ghaill** (ed.), *Understanding Masculinities*, Milton Keynes: Open University Press

43 See for instance, **M. Kimmel** (1996) *Manhood in America: A cultural history*, New York: The Free Press

44 **R. Connell** (1995) *Masculinities*; and (2000) *The Men and the Boys*, both Cambridge: Polity

45 **R. Connell** (1998) 'Masculinities and globalisation', *Men and Masculinities*, Vol. 1, No. 1

46 A useful and straightforward framework for planning projects at community level which can be employed in interventions that target men is the 'Gender Analysis Matrix'. See **C. March, I. Smyth, M. Mukhopadhyay** (1999) *A Guide to Gender-Analysis Frameworks*, Oxford: Oxfam GB

47 **N. Kabeer** (1994) *Reversed Realities: Gender hierarchies in development thought*, London: Verso

Chapter 3

1 See for example **P. Alcock, C. Beatty, S. Fothergill, R. MacMillan, S. Yeandle** (eds.) *Work to Welfare: how men become detached from the labour market*, Cambridge: Cambridge University Press (in press); **B. Stafford, C. Heaver, K. Ashworth, C. Bates, R. Walker, S. McKay, H. Trickey** (1999) *Work and Young Men*, York: Joseph Rowntree Foundation

2 See for example **F. Porter, I. Smyth, C. Sweetman** (eds.) (1999) *Gender Works: Oxfam experience in policy and practice*, Oxford: Oxfam GB

3 See **Working with Men** http://www.wwm-uk.freeuk.com/

Chapter 4

1 'Households Below Average Income Statistics', 11 April 2002, Office for National Statistics

2 **M. Rahman, G. Palmer, P. Kenway** (2001) *Monitoring Poverty and Social Exclusion 2001*, New Policy Institute, York: Joseph Rowntree Foundation

3 Some commentators argue, however, that further progress in reducing child poverty will be much harder to achieve. See for instance **D. Piachaud, H. Sutherland**, 'Child poverty: progress and prospects', *New Economy*, June 2001

4 The Sure Start programme aims to improve the health and well-being of children under four and their families. By 2004, there will be at least 500 Sure Start local programmes, concentrated in neighbourhoods where a high proportion of children are living in poverty. The Government

invested £452 million in Sure Start during the period 1999-2000 to 2001-2002. The Spending Review in July 2000 announced an extra £580 million for Sure Start over the period April 2001 to March 2004.

5 These are: The New Deal for Young People, for those aged 18-24 and unemployed for at least 6 months; The New Deal for the Long-Term Unemployed, for those aged 25 plus; The New Deal for Lone Parents; The New Deal for Partners; The New Deal for Disabled People; and The New Deal for People Aged 50 and Above

6 **J. Hills** (2000) *Taxation for the Enabling State*, CASE paper 41, Centre for Analysis of Social Exclusion, STICERD, London School of Economics

7 A range of further changes was also announced in the 2002 Budget, including an extra £4bn for public spending in 2003; a minimum-income guarantee for pensioners; extra support for families; introduction of the Step-up scheme (a pilot project for high-unemployment areas); mandatory work-preparation courses for the long-term jobless; and extension of tax credits covering childless couples.

8 **C. Howarth, P. Kenway G. Palmer** (2001) *Responsibility for All: A National Strategy for Social Inclusion*, London: New Policy Institute and Fabian Society; **Oxfam GB** (April 2001), 'Submission to Department of Social Security: UK Government National Action Plan against poverty and social exclusion'

9 By October 2001, as a result of personal tax and benefit measures, on average women were £440 a year better-off and men £225 a year better-off, compared with 1997. House of Commons, *Hansard Written Answers,* 13 March 2001, cols. 555-6W

10 From 2003 a new child tax credit will replace the child-related elements of income support, the working families' tax credit, disabled person's tax credit, children's tax credit, and income-based jobseekers' allowance. Unlike the children's tax credit, it will be paid to the main carer (in practice, most often the mother).

11 **J. Rubery, K. Rake** (2000) *Gender Impact Assessment in the UK*, European Commission's Expert Group on Gender and Employment, www.umist.ac.uk/management/ewerc/egge/egge_publications/ GIA_UK.pdf

12 **Low Pay Commission** (2000) 'The National Minimum Wage: the story so far', second report, London: The Stationery Office

13 **H. Robinson** (2001) 'Wrong Side of the Track? The impact of the minimum wage on gender pay gaps in Britain', presentation at the Centre for Economic Performance, Conference on 'National Minimum Wage: the 21st Century', SEP

14 The main and youth rates of the minimum wage will be increased by 10 pence per hour from October 2002, to £4.20 and £3.60 respectively.

15 J. Rubery, K. Rake (2000) *op. cit.*

16 'Gender mainstreaming' aims to achieve gender equality by bringing this perspective into everyday policy making, and by complementing more traditional approaches to promoting gender equality, such as legislation and positive action.

17 **J. Squires, M. Wickham-Jones** (2001) *Women in Parliament: A Comparative Analysis*, EOC Research Discussion Series, Manchester: EOC

18 **J. Squires, M. Wickham-Jones** (2002) 'Mainstreaming in Westminster and Whitehall: From Labour's Ministry for Women to the Women and Equality Unit', *Parliamentary Affairs*, Vol. 55 No 1, January 2002, Hansard Society, Oxford University Press

19 **Women's Unit** (1998) *Policy Appraisal for Equal Treatment*, London: Cabinet Office

20 *The Policy Appraisal for Equal Treatment* guidelines were introduced in November 1998, led by the Home Office, Department for Education and Employment, and the Minister for Women. They were intended to help civil servants check how policies or programmes would affect, either directly or indirectly, various groups of people (e.g. women and men, disabled people, and those from different ethnic groups); to identify any adverse differential impact and decide whether it can be justified in policy terms, even if it is legally permissible; and to take action, if necessary.

21 **P. Chaney, R. Fevre** (2002) 'How Significant has been the National Assembly for Wales' Statutory Duty to Promote Equality of Opportunity?', presented at seminar on mainstreaming, 7 February 2002, Cardiff

22 **F. MacKay, K. Bilton** (2000) 'Learning from Experience: Lessons in Mainstreaming Equal Opportunities', Governance of Scotland Forum, Edinburgh: University of Edinburgh

23 Although the government took the important step of launching a Gender Statistics Users Group in 1998 (with support from the Office of National Statistics, the Women's Unit, and the Equal Opportunities Commission), disaggregated statistics are still not routinely published across departments.

Chapter 5

1 **HM Treasury** (1999) *Tackling Poverty and Extending Opportunity*

2 In line with this approach, at EU level the European Employment Strategy requires Member States to develop and update regular National Action Plans on Employment.

3 For example, **R. Lister**, speech at the Fabian Society 'Transforming Britain' Conference, January 2001; **R. Levitas** (1998) *The Inclusive Society?: Social Exclusion and New Labour*, Basingstoke: Macmillan

4 **R. Levitas** (1998) *ibid.*

5   P. Alcock, C. Beatty, S. Fothergill, R. MacMillan, S. Yeandle (eds.)
    Work to Welfare: how men become detached from the labour market,
    Cambridge: Cambridge University Press (in press)

6   'Reasons for economic inactivity: by gender' Spring 2000, Labour Force
    Survey, Office for National Statistics

7   R. Berthoud (1998) *Disability Benefits: A review of the issues and options
    for reform*, York: Joseph Rowntree Foundation

8   B. Stafford, C. Heaver, K. Ashworth, C. Bates, R. Walker, S. McKay and
    H. Trickey (1999) *Work and Young Men*, York: Joseph Rowntree
    Foundation

9   R. Berthoud (1999) *Young Caribbean Men and the Labour Market:
    A comparison with other ethnic groups*, York: Joseph Rowntree Foundation

10 The Gurnos Centre is a local-authority project – a New Deal service-
    provider with a furniture-recycling centre and carpentry workshops.
    It is also establishing an environmental task force to act as an
    intermediate labour market between New Deal and the open market.

11 Registered unemployment is very low in Merthyr, but only because of
    high levels of sickness. Many men under age 50 are claiming benefits.

12 Fathers Plus (2000) *Including Fathers*

13 L. Johnston, R. MacDonald, P. Mason, L. Ridley, C. Webster (2000)
    Snakes & Ladders: Young people, transitions and social exclusion, Bristol:
    Policy Press; T. Lloyd (1999) *Young Men, the Job Market and Gendered
    Work*, York Publishing Services: Joseph Rowntree Foundation;
    J. Graham, B. Bowling (1995) *Young People and Crime*, Home Office
    Research Study no. 145, London: Home Office

14 J. Millar (2000) *Keeping Track of Welfare Reform: The New Deal Programmes*,
    York: Joseph Rowntree Foundation

15 T.Lloyd (1999) *Young Men's Attitudes to Gender and Work*, York: Joseph
    Rowntree Foundation

16 L. McDowell (2001) *Young Men Leaving School: white, working-class
    masculinity*, York: Joseph Rowntree Foundation/Youth Work Press

17 H. Rolfe (1999) *Gender Equality and the Careers Service*, Research
    Discussion Series, Manchester: Equal Opportunities Commission

18 L. McDowell (2001) *op. cit.*

19 New Deal 50plus is directed towards people aged 50 and over, who
    have been out of work for six months or more, and wish to return to
    employment. Participation in the programme is voluntary. The main
    elements of it are one-to-one support with job search from a New Deal
    Personal Adviser (NDPA), a wage top-up (Employment Credit) for those
    who find work for one year, and a Training Grant.

20 J. Kodz, J. Eccles (2001) *Evaluation of New Deal 50 Plus: Qualitative
    evidence from clients: Second Phase*, Employment Service

21 J. Millar (2000), *op. cit.*

22 **V. McGivney** (1999) *Excluded Men: Men who are missing from education and training*, Leicester: National Institute of Adult Continuing Education

23 *Ibid.*

24 Since spring 2000 The Health Action Zone Innovation Fund, set up by the Department of Health, has been supporting projects which aim to reduce health inequalities by finding innovative ways of targeting health concerns in selected regions. It is envisaged that successful projects will be replicable elsewhere in the country.

25 Figures from Nacro and Payback, www.nacro.org.uk and www.payback.org.uk

Chapter 6

1 *Our Healthier Nation* (1998) 'A Contract for Health: A Consultation Paper', Cm3852, London: The Stationery Office

2 **R. Mitchell, D. Dorling, M. Shaw** (2000) *Inequalities in Life and Death: What if Britain were more equal?*, Bristol: The Policy Press

3 **Men's Health Forum** Press Release, 16 May 2000, available from www.menshealthforum.org.uk/newsandevents/pr-inequalities.htm

4 *The Independent Inquiry into Inequalities in Health* (1998) London: The Stationery Office

5 *Ibid.*

6 **R. Wilkinson** (1996) *Unhealthy Societies: the afflictions of inequality*, London: Routledge

7 **N. Davidson** (1999) *Young Men and Mental Health*, London: Working With Men

8 **T. Lloyd, S. Forrest** (2001) *Boys' and Young Men's Health: literature and practice review*, London: Health Development Agency; and **T. Lloyd and S. Forrest** (2001) *Boys' and Young Men's Health: Practice examples*, London: Health Development Agency

9 **National Statistics** (2001) *Social Focus on Men*, London: The Stationery Office

10 **Department of Health** (2000) 'The NHS Plan: A Plan for Investment. A Plan for Reform', available on www.nhs.uk/nhsplan

11 **Department of Health** (2001) 'Tackling Health Inequalities: Consultation on a plan for delivery', available on www.doh.gov.uk/healthinequalities

12 **Department of Health** (2001) 'National Strategy for Sexual Health and HIV', available on www.doh.gov.uk/nshs/strategy

13 A rolling programme of National Service Frameworks has been developed since 1998 to set standards and to support implementation of policy. They currently cover cancer, mental health, coronary heart disease, and older people. Further frameworks are under development in relation to diabetes, renal services, children's services, and neurological conditions.

14 **J. Coleman, J. Schofield** (2000) *Key Data on Adolescence*, Brighton: Trust for the Study of Adolescence

15 **H. Meltzer, B. Gill, M. Petticrew, K. Hinds** (1995) *The Prevalence of Psychiatric Morbidity amongst Adults Living in Private Households*, OPCS Survey of Psychiatric Morbidity in Great Britain, Report 1, London: The Stationery Office

16 **P.M. Prior** (1999) *Gender and Mental Health*, London: Macmillan

17 **S. Fernando, D. Ndegwa, M. Wilson** (1998) *Forensic Psychiatry, Race and Culture*, London: Routledge

18 **National Statistics** (2001) *Social Focus on Men*, London: The Stationery Office

19 **A. Katz, A. Buchanan, A. McCoy** (1999) *Young Men Speak Out*, The Samaritans

20 **Men's Health Forum** (2000) 'Young Men and Suicide', available online at www.menshealthforum.org.uk

21 **N. Davidson** (1999) *op. cit.*

22 **Social Exclusion Unit** (1999) *Teenage Pregnancy*, Cm4342, London: Cabinet Office

23 **National Assembly for Wales** (2000) *A Strategic Framework for Promoting Sexual Health in Wales*, London: The Stationery Office

24 Report of the Consultation Day on the Sexual Health Strategy for Wales, 16 February 2000, fpa Cymru

25 **Department of Health** (2001), 'Sexual Health and HIV Strategy: A Consultation Document', London: Department of Health

26 **Sex Education Forum** (1997) *Supporting the Needs of Boys and Young Men in Sex and Relationships Education*, Factsheet 11, London: National Children's Bureau

27 **S. Blake, J. Laxton** (1998) *Strides: A Practical Guide to Sex and Relationships Education with Young Men*, London: Family Planning Association

28 **Men's Health Forum 2000** (2000), interview with Yvette Cooper, Minister for Public Health, 19 September 2000 www.menshealthforum.org.uk/newsandevents/yvetteinterviewfull.htm

29 **P. Baker** (2001) speech at Oxfam GB seminar on Men and Poverty, Oxford, 20 March 2001

Chapter 7

1 **R. Connell** (1995) *Masculinities*, Cambridge: Polity

2 **M. Kimmel** (2000) *The Gendered Society*, New York: Oxford University Press

3   **E. Stanko** Domestic Violence in the UK', British Crime Survey Statistics www.domesticviolencedata.org/5_research/count/count.htm

4   **E. Stanko** *et al.* (1998) *Taking Stock: What Do We Know about Violence?* Swindon: ESRC Violence Research Programme

5   Report of the Commission on Children and Violence (1995) *Children and Violence*, London: Calouste Gulbenkian Foundation

6   **A. Cornwall, N. Lindisfarne** (eds.) (1994) *Dislocating Masculinity: Comparative Ethnographies*, London: Routledge

7   **Women's Unit** (1999) *Living Without Fear: An Integrated Approach to Tackling Violence against Women*, London: Women's Unit and Cabinet Office

8   **C. Humphreys, G. Hester, A. Hague, H. Mullender, P. Abrahams, P. Lowe** (2000) *From Good Intentions to Good Practice: Mapping services working with families where there is domestic violence*, York: Joseph Rowntree Foundation

9   For further details, see **Change** ' Men's Programme' www.changeweb.org.uk/change_mens'_programme.htm

10 **R. Dobash, E. Dobash, K. Cavanagh, R. Lewis** (1999) 'A research evaluation of British programmes for violent men', *Journal of Social Policy* 28(2)

11 **C. Humphreys,** *et al.* (2000) *op. cit.*

12 The 'Duluth' model seeks to hold men responsible for their violent behaviour, through programmes which focus directly on men's need to change. Couple-counselling and mediation are deemed inappropriate, as they may inadvertently or otherwise, deflect attention from male responsibility.

13 **Ahimsa** (1999) 'Concerns over the Current Development of UK Domestic Violence Perpetrator Programmes', discussion paper presented to the Women's Unit/Home Office, www.ahimsa.org.uk

14 **D. Morran** (1999) 'Violent men: terrifying others, scared of themselves?' *Working With Men* 1999 (2): 3-5

15 **D. Potts** (1996) *Why Do Men Commit Most Crime? : Focusing on masculinity in a prison group*, West Yorkshire: Probation Service

16 **B. Campbell** (1993) *Goliath: Britain's Dangerous Places*, London: Methuen

17 **A. Underdown** (1998) 'Strategies for Effective Offender Supervision: Report of the HMIP What Works project', London: Home Office

18 **J. Jenkins** (1994) *Men, Masculinity and Offending*, London: Inner London Probation Service and London Action Trust

19 **K. Harland** (2002) '"Everyday life": developing youth work practice with young men in Northern Ireland around the theme of violence', *Working With Young Men*, Volume 1, January 2002

20 **S. Ruxton** (1996) 'Boys won't be boys: tackling the roots of male delinquency', in T. Lloyd and T. Wood (eds.) *What Next for Men?* London: Working With Men

21 **S. Williams, J. Seed, A. Mwau** (1995) *The Oxfam Gender Training Manual*, Oxford: Oxfam GB

22 **National Statistics** (2001) *Social Focus on Men*, London: The Stationery Office

23 **E. Stanko, K. Hobdell** (1993) 'Assault on men: masculinity and male victimisation', *British Journal of Criminology*, Vol. 33(3)

Chapter 8

1 **C. Murray** (1990) *The Emerging British Underclass*, London: IEA Health and Welfare Unit

2 **N. Dennis, G. Erdos** (1992) *Families without Fatherhood*, London: IEA Health and Welfare Unit

3 There are various conceptualisations of what is meant by 'father involvement' (a relatively new phrase in the literature). For example, Russell identifies six core areas: employment and family financial support; day-to-day care of and interaction with children; child management and socialisation; household work; maintaining relationships between care-givers; and parental commitment and investment. (See **G. Russell** (1999) *Primary Caregiving Fathers*, in **M.E. Lamb** (ed.), *Nontraditional Families*, 2nd edition, Hillsdale, NJ: Lawrence Erlbaum.) See also **A. Burgess, S. Ruxton** (1996) *Men and Their Children: Proposals for Public Policy*, London: IPPR

4 **F. Williams** 'Troubled masculinities: fatherhood', in J. Popay, J. Hearn, J. Edwards (1998) *Men, Gender Divisions and Welfare*, London/New York: Routledge

5 **B. Campbell** (1993) *Goliath: Britain's Dangerous Places*, London: Methuen

6 **J. Scourfield, M. Drakeford** (2001) *New Labour and the Politics of Masculinity*, Paper 13, Working Paper Series, School of Social Sciences, Cardiff University

7 **C. Lewis** (2000) 'A Man's Place in the Home: Fathers and Families in the UK', Foundations 440, Joseph Rowntree Foundation, www.jrf.org.uk/knowledge/findings/foundations/440.htm

8 **E. Flouri, A. Buchanan** *Fathering and Child Outcomes*, Oxford: Oxford University Press (forthcoming)

9 **European Commission Network on Childcare** (1996) *A Review of Services for Young Children in the European Union 1990-1995*, Equal Opportunities Unit, Directorate General for Employment, Industrial Relations and Social Affairs, Brussels: European Commission

10 **National Statistics**, Labour Force Survey, Spring 2000

11 **G. Russell** (2001) 'Adopting a global perspective on fatherhood', in B. Pease and K. Pringle, *A Man's World?: Changing Men's Practices in a Globalized World*, London/New York: Zed Books

12 **R.Taylor** (2001) *The Future of Work–Life Balance*, Swindon: ESRC

13 **J. Warin, Y. Solomon, C. Lewis, W. Langford** (1999) *Fathers, Work and Family Life*, London: Family Policy Studies Centre

14 **J. Bradshaw, C. Stimson, C. Skinner, J. Williams** (1999) *Absent Fathers?*, London: Routledge

15 **Gingerbread** (2001) *Becoming Visible: Focus on lone fathers*, London: Gingerbread

16 **L. Haas, P. Hwang** (2000) 'Programs and policies promoting women's economic equality and men's sharing of child care in Sweden', in **Haas** *et al.* (eds), *Organisational Change and Gender Equality: International Perspectives on Fathers and Mothers at the Workplace*, Thousand Oaks CA: Sage

17 **Gingerbread** (2001) *op. cit.*

18 If the non-resident parent earns between £200 and £2,000 per week after tax, national insurance, and pension contributions, he will have to pay 15 per cent for one child, 20 per cent for two, and 25 per cent for three or more. The other parent's income will no longer be taken into account, but the amount paid will be reduced by up to 25 per cent if the paying parent is supporting children in a new relationship.

19 **R. Pickford** (1999) *Fathers, Marriage and the Law*, London: Family Policy Studies Centre

20 **J. Edwards** 'Screening out men' in J. Popay, J. Hearn and J. Edwards (1998) *Men, Gender Divisions and Welfare*, London: Routledge.

21 **K. Pringle** (1998) 'Men and childcare: policy and practice', in Popay *et al.* (eds.), *op. cit.*

22 **C. Cameron, P. Moss, C. Owen** (1999) *Men in the Nursery*, London: Paul Chapman Publishing

23 **A. Burgess, S. Ruxton** (1996) *op. cit.*

24 **D. Ghate, C. Shaw, N. Hazel** (2000), *Fathers and Family Centres*, London: Policy Research Bureau

25 **C. Cameron, P. Moss, C. Owen** (1999) *op. cit.*

26 **Gingerbread** (2001) *op. cit.*

27 **A. Burgess** (2000) *Fathers Figure*, London: Institute for Public Policy Research

28 **D. Ghate**, *et al.* (2000) *op. cit.*

29 **C. Lewis** (2000) *op. cit.*

30 **Gingerbread** (2001) *op. cit.*

31 **S. Speak, S. Cameron, R. Gilroy** (1997) *Young Single Fathers: Participation in Fatherhood – Barriers and Bridges*, York: Joseph Rowntree Foundation

Chapter 9

1   C. March, I. Smyth, M. Mukhopadhyay (1999) *A Guide to Gender-Analysis Frameworks*, Oxford: Oxfam GB

2   *Ibid.*

3   J. Squires, M. Wickham-Jones (2002) 'Mainstreaming in Westminster and Whitehall: From Labour's Ministry for Women to the Women and Equality Unit', *Parliamentary Affairs*, Vol. 55 No 1, January 2002, Hansard Society, Oxford University Press

4   European Commission (2000) 'Towards a Community Framework Strategy on Gender Equality (2001-2005)', Communication from the Commission to the Council, the European Parliament, The Economic and Social Committee, and the Committee of the Regions, Brussels 7/6/2000

5   Equal Opportunities Commission (1997) *Mainstreaming Gender Equality in Local Government*, Manchester: Equal Opportunities Commission

6   P. Alcock, C. Beatty, S. Fothergill, R. MacMillan, S. Yeandle (eds.) *Work to Welfare: how men become detached from the labour market*, Cambridge: Cambridge University Press (in press)

7   M. Ryan (2000) *Working With Fathers*, Department of Health, Abingdon: Radcliffe Medical Press

8   Working With Men (2001) *Boys' and Young Men's Health: Literature and practice review*, London: Health Development Agency

9   Social Exclusion Unit (1998) *Rough Sleepers*, Cm4008, The Stationery Office

10 G. Pearson (1983) *A History of Respectable Fears*, London: Macmillan

11 S. Frosch, A. Phoenix, R. Pattman (2002) *Young Masculinities: Understanding Boys in Contemporary Societies*, Basingstoke: Palgrave

12 N. Davidson (1999) *Young Men and Mental Health*, London: Working With Men

13 D. Molloy, J. Richie (2000) *New Deal for Long Term Unemployed People: Findings from a Qualitative Study among Participants*, Employment Service

14 K. Green, I. Trafford (2002), 'The men's group – words in action', *Working With Young Men*, Volume 1, January 2002

15 T. Lloyd (1997) *Let's Get Changed Lads: Developing work with boys and young men*, London: Working With Men

16 NCVCCO (2000) 'Fathers at the Centre: Family centres, fathers and working with men', Conference Report 2 March 2000; B. Kissman (2001) 'Are We Shutting Out Fathers?', Conference Report 15 March 2001, NCVCCO

17 M. Ryan (2000) *op. cit.*

18 C. Cameron, P. Moss, C. Owen (1999) *Men in the Nursery*, London: Paul Chapman Publishing

19 **Working With Men** (2001) *op. cit.*

20 **C. Cameron**, *et al. op. cit.*

21 **J. Jensen** (1996) *Men as Workers in Childcare Services*, European Commission Network on Childcare and other Measures to reconcile Employment and Family Responsibilities, Brussels: European Equal Opportunities Unit

22 **R. Crompton** (1997) *Women and Work in Modern Britain*, Oxford: Oxford University Press

23 **DfEE** (2000) *Good Practice for EYDC Partnerships, Recruitment Strategies for Childcare Workers*, Nottingham: Department for Education and Employment

24 **DfEE** (2001) *Early Years Development and Childcare Partnership Planning Guidance 2001-2002*, Nottingham: Department for Education and Employment

25 **J. Jensen** (1996) *op. cit.*

26 **Working With Men** (2001) *op. cit.*

27 **National Statistics** (2001) *Social Focus on Men*, London: The Stationery Office

28 **L. Burghes, L. Clarke, N. Cronin** (1997) *Fathers and Fatherhood in Britain*, Family Policy Studies Centre

29 **K. Pringle** (2000), 'UK National Report on Research on Men's Practices', Workpackage 1, www.cromenet.org

30 **Ø. Holter** 'A Revolt for Equality? On men, women and gender discrimination', paper at Men and Gender Equality conference, Orebro, Sweden, 16 March 2001, www.cromenet.org

Appendix

Projects, organisations, and individuals contacted during Oxfam research

Organisation	Name	Internet
ENGLAND AND WALES		
Men's Health Forum	Peter Baker	www.menshealthforum.org.uk
LEAP, North London	Tunde Banjuko	www.leap.org.uk
Fathers Direct	David Bartlett Adrienne Burgess	www.fathersdirect.com
Sex Education Forum	Simon Blake	www.ncb.org.uk/sef
Detached Youth Work Project, York	David Blockley	
fpa Cymru, Cardiff	Alun Burge Socrates Siskos	www.fpa.org.uk
CREST, Salford	Colette Carol	
The Skills Centre, Gurnos, Merthyr Tydfil	Robert Cornwall	
Gingerbread	Margaret Creer	www.gingerbread.org.uk
National Family and Parenting Institute	Clem Henricson	www.nfpi.org
Recharge, Cardiff	Colin Heyman	www.fusionpartnership.co.uk
Fathers Plus, Newcastle	Joy Higginson	
New Pathways, Merthyr Tydfil	Libby Jones	
Working With Men	Trefor Lloyd Neil Davidson	www.workingwithmen.org
42nd Street, Manchester	Donovan Powell Richard Moosbally	
Equal Opportunities Commission	David Perfect	www.eoc.org.uk

Independent Consultant	Mary Ryan	
CALM	Pippa Sargent	www.thecalmzone.net
Let's Get Serious, Hulme, Manchester	Richard Strittmater	www.letsgetserious.com
MIND	George Stewart	www.mind.org.uk
Navigator Men's Development Programme	James Traeger	www.navigator-network.com
YMCA Dads and Lads	Dirk Utterdijk	www.ymca.org.uk

SCOTLAND

CHANGE		www.changeweb.org.uk
Barlinnie Prison (Social Work Unit)		
Dunfermline Area Abuse Survivors Project		
Lone Father Project		www.meninchildcare.com/index2.htm
The Simon Community, Glasgow	Alistair Fergusson	
Men's Health Forum Scotland	Alastair Pringle	www.menshealthforum.org.uk/mhfscotland
Men's Health Highland		www.men4life.org

Index